Jonny Baker
Michael Moynagh
Ian Adams
Max Harris
Steve Collins
Emma Major
Colin Heber-Percy
Anna Ruddick
Rachel Griffiths
Nicola Slee
John Drane
Michael Northcott
Cathy Ross

future
*7*present

embodying a better world **now**

Contents

future present

jonny baker

>>There are so many areas of life where it feels as though the system is broken or stuck, that it needs to change, that we need to imagine and build something different. This is true of political life, farming methods, our dependency on oil which is depleting and overheating the planet, the growing disparity between rich and poor, how we organise society, how we care for those pushed to the margins of society, how we celebrate diversity, and how the church organises as communities of followers of Jesus.

When faced with the need to change there are a few possible responses. This zine is not that interested in postures of denial or defence. I saw a a wonderful photo typifying this sort of response with a crowd of people on a beach all with their heads buried in the sand - it was a protest at the denial of climate change. I took the self portrait photo above when I was out walking near Bath on a disused railway track. I called it 'waiting for the train that no longer arrives'. In many areas of life where the world has changed and the flow of life moved elsewhere people keep doing things that once worked and flourished rather than move elsewhere. This is not necessarily denial - it can simply be a failure to notice the change that has taken place all around and then suddenly it feels too late, or perhaps it is a blindness or an ignorance.

We are assuming here that the reader is interested in change and newness wanting to make a better world, to make good, to enable flourishing, to come up with creative solutions. We won't be spending much time making the case for change.

A common practice around change is to look at the way things have been done and to tweak and adjust them. This works well to improve existing solutions. But where it doesn't work is where the system itself needs to change. Something much more radical is called for.

In their book *The Radical Imagination: Social Movement Research In The Age Of Austerity* Alex Khasnabish and Max Haiven give an example from university research which is the field they work in. They don't like the way university life is organised and structured. So they say what is needed is prefigurative research. What they mean by this is that the first task is to imagine a university that is differently organised in a way that leads to flourishing. Then the research in the present should be designed and done on the basis of that imagined future university and not on the basis of tweaking the present way of organising, i.e. it prefigures a different world. They work with social activists and movements to work in this way. They facilitate groups where the task is to dream and imagine different futures and then ask 'so what' for how we act in the present now. They have discovered that this builds communities of resilience and social movements that are fecund ecologies ripe with possibility. In using research to gather people in this way they find that participants gets loads out of it and thank them for it. But they also say that they would not have made the space for reflection and imagination that has led to change if they had not been invited into a space to do so!

Future present takes that idea, that approach to change. It can be applied to any area of life and culture. The first task is to imagine the future and then the second task is to act in the present on the basis of that imagined future, to make the future present, to embody a better world now. The reflections in this zine are quite macro - planet, church, city. But it actually gets just as interesting when drilled down to something very focused and local - a village school, a business, sharing work and parenting in a marriage, what to do about the 8 churches in a deanery, 6 families stressed out on work and paying the bills exploring how they might live differently together.

Future present is a play on a tense. It says something will have happened. The future is present. Life gets so busy and focused on the immediate that it's much easier to live and act in the past continuous tense unable to change or shift out of old ways of doing, thinking, being. It does take some kind of intervention, space and intentionality to have a different kind of conversation. That was the idea behind a day we held where we invited contributors to take an area and do this kind of imagining. This is what we said on the blurb for that day:

Everything created was at some point an idea, a dream of someone somewhere. Another world is always possible, always dream-able. Always right in front of us. How can we realise the future now?

Join us for a day of imagining together how we can make God's dreams for our world come true: for our planet, for our cities, for society, for the church, for our neighbourhoods, for us. Now...

We are currently looking for people who want to contribute creatively to this conversation. This could be in relation to any area – mission, the workplace, the economy, education, sexuality, community, you name it. We're calling on speakers, poets, artists, photographers, filmmakers, writers, musicians, storytellers, architects, activists, prophets, theologians, builders, social entrepreneurs, community developers, advocates for justice to gather, present ideas and dream together.

The day will be built around our dreams. And our dreams will build our todays. The future is at hand. It's time to change tense.

There is a great tradition of this sort of thinking in theology. It's what the prophets did. They grieved for the way the world was broken enabling the shedding of tears where people had become numb to the reigning empire's way of dong things. Grief leads to newness. Then they imagined a different future through their poetry and art - another world where swords are beaten into ploughshares, where there is no sorrow and sighing, where the healing of nations takes place, where justice dwells, a banquet where all are at the table together and there is no exclusion, there is a new heaven and earth. Jesus called this future the kingdom of God and announced the future present when he said 'the kingdom of God is here', and proceeded to live life in the light of that incoming future.

Whilst this all sounds pretty easy and straightforward, the bad news is that Jesus got killed! It turns out the empires and systems have plenty of people who have vested interests in the way things are, in the status quo and they do quite nicely out of a world of business as usual. So making the future present is difficult. There are lots of accounts of inspiring people - innovators, entrepreneurs, prophets, artists, saints - who changed the world. In almost every case the ideas that they had got rubbished at the time and they are effectively labelled as heretics within whatever community or institution they are in. They saw something that others couldn't see. And yet they somehow persisted to give those ideas legs and make them reality.

I have been reading *We Do Things Differently: Outsiders Rebooting Our World* by Mark Stevenson in which the author has sought out people who have come up with solutions to some of the crises the world is facing. They range from methods of growing rice that increase yield without use of chemicals that erode soil to designing an engine that drives a piston based on going from liquid gas which is really cold to air and has a by-product of refrigeration. The latter has the dual benefit of helping food be refrigerated so there is less waste and emitting zero carbon. In every case you would think that the farming community or scientific community would welcome these brilliant innovations. But I found the book a sobering reminder of how particularly change that has to imagine a different paradigm or world in which its innovation makes sense is invariably fraught with opposition initially.

So for the future to be made present as well as the dreaming and imagining there is likely to need to be some nous about process of change. Alongside imagination there will need to be some tactics and strategy to navigate the building of whatever is dreamed alongside some tenacity. And there is a sort of received wisdom in anthropology which looks at change that the new is often best done with some distance from the old. Gerald Arbuckle suggests that the new belongs elsewhere and needs some distance and protection from the powers that be if it is likely to have a chance to succeed along with some institutional advocates who fully get and support the innovating pioneer. Margaret Wheatley and Deborah Frieze in *Walk Out Walk On: A Learning Journey Into Communities Daring To Live The Future Now* similarly map a change process where those seeing new worlds need to not be in the old system if they are to have the space to embody a different kind of world out of the future they imagine. And very much like the process in *The Radical Imagination* it is the friends on the journey with them together who provide a community of supportive pioneers that creates a different kind of ecosystem where new possibilities and imagination run freely rather than being resisted.

This is not to devalue the present or the past. There is great gift and treasure in both. And of course newness or change for its own sake is not worth much. And it's by no means everyone's task to dream the future. But there are those seers, artists, prophets, poets, pioneers, innovators, entrepreneurs, whose gift and call is to dream new worlds and make paths where there are no paths that others will be able to follow later.

The reflections here are really inspiring and varied. We hope they catalyse some conversation and new ideas for others. But above all we hope that it might lead to some small groups who get together over a meal or a drink for some friendship and conversation who dare to imagine future present in a whole range of areas of life and culture. The process we are suggesting is pretty simple and could be summarised in three steps:

1. Get some people together.
2. Pick something you want to see changed and imagine a different future.
3. Design the present on the basis of that future to make the future present.

Bon voyage!

Bio:

Jonny Baker leads the pioneer training at the Church Mission Society where he is director of mission education - see pioneer.churchmissionsociety.org . He is also a speaker, writer, photographer, musician, lay pioneer, and loves all things creative - he blogs at jonnybaker.blogs.com

---

and

Every Journey St.
step, ENJOY

THE

confirm

♡ + ✝ =

Live strong be happy

DESTINY IS
THE NEW
WHITE - S

Future present is a play on a tense. It says something will have happened. The future is present.

Jonny Baker

innovating the future

michael moynagh

>>Innovation is what happens when God's future comes head to head with the present. The promised kingdom transforms the world through innovation - a process that changes the rules of the game for doing something.

The rules may change radically. The first Messy Church radically changed the rules of the game for all-age worship. Or they may change incrementally: Messy Church leaders might change the sequence of craft activities, worship and food. Whether radical or incremental, innovation is the Spirit's vehicle for pulling the present toward God's future.

I would like to offer a framework for thinking about innovation. The framework is drawn from the research literature on entrepreneurship, design thinking and on complexity theory (the study of how order, pattern and structure can arise within complex systems). It is also based on ten case studies of people who have innovated new forms of Christian community.

The framework describes six processes of innovation. They are not sequential, they overlap and they reinforce each other. They are far from the only way of thinking about innovation, and complement other approaches.

Dissatisfaction

The first process is dissatisfaction. Innovation does not happen unless there is dissatisfaction with the status quo. No one would do anything new unless they were discontent with the present. Perhaps the present isn't working. Or perhaps they can see better ways of doing something. The person feels dissatisfied because the present could be improved.

That was Caroline's experience. She was a school teacher in northwest London. The local population had changed, with a growing number of people from ethnic minority backgrounds. Caroline felt frustrated because her local church had so little contact with this changing population. Her discontent fuelled a determination to do something about it.

If you like, innovation starts with 'holy discontent' or 'prophetic discontent'. It begins with a dissatisfaction that says, "The situation could be better". The old must be revealed as inadequate before the new is born. This is a challenge to leaders who believe that the main task of management is to keep everyone happy. If you want improvement, you need some people not to be happy.

Exploration

A second process is exploration. An innovator - or more likely an innovating team - explores how something new might work within their context. Caroline, for example, began to explore how her church might make connections with its new neighbours. How might her church 'change the rules of the game' to build relationships with recent migrants nearby?

Caroline explored in three ways. First, she started with what she'd got - who she was, what she knew and who she knew. So who was she? She was a primary school teacher. What did she know? She knew that many of the mothers of her children could not speak English, or could not speak it well. She also knew how to teach. She wondered if she could use her teaching skills to help these mothers learn better English? Who did Caroline know? As well as some of the mothers, she knew people in the church who might be willing to help her.

Secondly, she began to ask herself "What if?" "What if I did this?" Or "What if I did that?" This is an important part of the exploring process. In *Design Thinking: Understanding How Designers Think and Work*, Nigel Cross describes how engineers, architects and other designers approach design problems by thinking about possible solutions. They keep asking "What if..." till a solution emerges.

Caroline was designing a solution to the problem of ethnic women not speaking English. So she began to think about possible solutions. One was to run a language course. But she realised that she would have to write course materials and set assignments, which would take more time than she had. She would also probably need qualified helpers, and these were not readily available. So she dismissed the idea. Eventually, she asked herself, "What if we run a weekly language café - invite the women to an English afternoon tea, sit them round tables, and invite them to discuss a topic in English."

I don't know whether she said "Wow!" at this point. But often when you repeatedly ask 'What if?' and the apparent answer finally pops into your head, you exclaim "Wow!" And then, as happened with Caroline, you try the idea to see if it will work. What if? What wows? What works?

Cross points out that experienced designers do not foreclose the "What if?" process too quickly. They keep options open to avoid missing a good idea. Neither do they give up too soon. Often you have to persevere, imagining one solution and then another, till you hit on a brainwave. This was true of Caroline, who continued to ask "What if?" after rejecting the language course. If she had not persevered, she might never have come up with the language café.

Thirdly, she listened carefully to the mainly Sri Lankan mothers she hoped to serve. She knew some of them through her teaching, and so quite a bit of this listening was implicit. She held conversations in her head. She imagined herself inviting these mothers to afternoon tea in the church hall. And as she did so, she realised that many of them would find it quite daunting. The church was not part of their housing estate. She decided to use the community hall instead. The facilities were not as convenient for her, but it was familiar territory for the women involved. Besides listening implicitly, Caroline consulted some of the women as her plans took shape.

She started with what she had, which meant that she didn't waste time coming up with ideas that were completely beyond the resources available to her; nor did she try to innovate in a field with which she was unfamiliar - she was able to build on her existing expertise. She kept thinking of possible solutions, which widened her thinking to embrace an unexpected possibility. And she listened carefully to check her idea would work and then to shape it round the women concerned. This is the essence of the exploration process.

Sense making

The third overlapping process is making sense - to yourself and to others - of the idea that begins to emerge. Why does this idea make sense to me? Why could it make sense to you? This is a more subtle process than coming up with a vision. It is about telling different, yet consistent stories to the people involved - stories that will connect with them and convince them.

Caroline told three stories to three different audiences. The first was to herself. She had read *Mission-Shaped Church*, the 2004 Church of England report that did much to put 'fresh expressions of church' on the map. She was very taken by its incarnational theology. So she told herself the story: "Just as the Son of God went out to the culture of first-century Palestine, so in a small way I am trying to go out to people round here from Sri Lanka."

To her local church, she told a slightly different story: "For over 100 years we have supported overseas mission. Overseas has now come to us. What are we going to do about it?" And to the Sri Lankan women she told a different story again. "We want to be good neighbours to you and welcome you to this part of London. We'd like to invite you to tea, and help you practice your English."

Each of these stories, consistent and with a common thread, connected to the tradition or history of its audience. Caroline's story to herself connected with her long-standing passion to see her church reaching out. Her story to the church connected with its tradition of supporting overseas mission. And her story to the Sri Lankan women connected to their recent history of arriving in the U.K.

Story telling is vital to the process of innovation, and many innovators and their teams do it instinctively. But might some of the stories be improved if innovators were more intentional about their story telling, and in particular about how they connect their stories to the different traditions and concerns of the audiences they address?

Amplification

The fourth process of innovation is amplification. It is the process by which the innovation takes root, grows and spreads. The innovation 'amplifies'. Obviously a good story helps with this, and so do good networks. An innovation will race through networks if people are well connected (and they like it!). But if people are not well connected, the innovation will spread more slowly.

Especially important is the role of connectors in these networks. A connector is someone who knows lots of other people and whose views are taken seriously.

In mission circles they are often known as 'people of peace'. They open doors to their friends and contacts. If you've got the support of a good connector, many of their friends, neighbours and relatives will hear about your innovation and perhaps show an interest.

Caroline was almost certainly something of a connector herself. As a teacher in the local primary school, she knew quite a few of the Sri Lankan families she wanted to reach. She was able to invite the mothers of the children she had taught. She also knew people in her church whom she could invite to volunteer.

Understanding the role of connectors is important. If the innovator or innovating team lacks the gift of making connections, the innovation is most likely to spread if a connector outside the team can be persuaded to introduce it to their networks. Where people are not well connected, which is true of some social settings, or if a connector cannot be found, innovators should not be discouraged if their innovation spreads slowly or ends up smaller than they hoped. This may be due not to a deficiency within the innovation, but to an inhospitable social context.

Of course, connectors on their own are not enough. They have to be so enthused by a sense-making story that they tell their networks.That's why story telling is so important. And that's why it is important to see these processes of innovation together. They overlap and feed into each other.

Edge of chaos

The fifth process is what some people describe as the edge of chaos. This refers to the boundary between order and chaos. If an innovation moves too far in the orderly direction, it tends to get prematurely fixed. Further development is stifled. Possibilities that might expand the innovation's potential are strangled. By contrast, when you move toward chaos, you move away from order toward fluidity and change. The danger is that you move too far in this direction - you fall over the cliff - and there is too much change. Things begin to fall apart. You end up in a state of chaos.

Innovators must keep a balance between order and change. They don't want to change too much too quickly. Otherwise people will feel overwhelmed - the venture feels too chaotic - and they refuse to help. Equally, innovators must beware of getting stuck. If they feel too content with their routines, they will miss opportunities to enhance the innovation. Getting the balance right is to be on the edge of chaos.

Caroline's language cafe could easily have got stuck. She and her volunteers settled into a weekly pattern. Every Thursday afternoon tea was served, guests were encouraged to discuss a topic in English, and the hall was cleared up afterwards. Caroline and her team might have become comfortable with the routine and with knowing that they were providing a useful service and, in a small way, a taste of the kingdom.

But Caroline was not content. She was open, indeed looking for something more. When I first met her at a training course, she described her language café and then said, "We've got a bit stuck. I don't know how to move to the next stage. I want to be able to share the gospel appropriately with the women, but we don't know how." Here was an attitude that was distinctly receptive to change. Caroline was leaning toward the edge of chaos.

I suggested that her team invite the women to submit prayer requests and offer to pray for them. Caroline took the suggestion back to her team, who decided to set up a prayer board. The women pinned their requests to the board, and then began talking about them. This raised the spiritual temperature of the café, which made it easier for the team to offer the café's guests an Alpha course at a different time of the week.

The café was developing its own weekly tradition - afternoon tea, discussion around tables and so on. But Caroline refused to be imprisoned by that tradition. She remained open to the possibility of further innovation to enhance the café's offering to its guests. Edge of chaos is about sitting on the boundary between being faithful to the emerging tradition of your innovation, and being open to more change.

Some people find this uncomfortable because they are not fully in control. Caroline was open to more, but didn't know what to do. She needed some outside stimulus, which was beyond her control. She felt a little frustrated because she couldn't find the answer. All she could do was to wait and ask questions. She didn't know where the answer would come from, nor even whether she would get an answer. But this willingness to live with uncertainty paid off. She was prepared to be surprised by an unexpected suggestion that took the café's journey to its next milestone.

So often leaders of innovation want to control what happens. They close down possibilities. In so doing, they impose too much order on their initiatives and risk missing out on fruitful further developments. We might think of this as stifling the Spirit. Leaving room for the Spirit to act includes living with uncertainty, leaving the future open and being prepared for change to come from an unexpected direction.

Transformation

The last process is transformation. Innovation brings about a degree of transformation among those involved. Some of Caroline's Sri Lankan women attended the Alpha course and then for several years continued to meet for regular bible study. Who knows what changes in outlook and behaviour resulted? One person was helped into a job through the café.

An important aspect of transformation, and one easily overlooked, is the effect of the innovation on the identities of those who lead it. Caroline's volunteers gained in confidence and began to see themselves as being more capable. Caroline's identity evolved. Before starting the café, she saw herself as someone in the pews with gifts. Successfully launching the café encouraged her to see herself as someone with the ability to lead something new. She began to see herself differently, and this confirmed her journey toward ordination.

Her local church began to see itself differently too. The congregation gained confidence in mission, and this may have contributed to the start of a Messy Church and of a debt counselling centre. The church still came from the same tradition, but it began to express that tradition in new ways. Thus innovation need not be a threat to tradition. It can enable a tradition to find a new lease of life.

Theological foundations

Through what theological lens might we view these six processes of innovation - dissatisfaction, exploration, sense making, amplification, edge of chaos and transformation? Some people suggest that we start with creation. God innovated when he created the universe. But Christians have traditionally said that this was creation from nothing. God used no pre-existing materials to form the universe.

This is not how innovators work. They don't start with nothing. They start with what they've got. Indeed, typically the essence of innovation, especially radical innovation, lies in bringing together two or more elements that were previously kept apart. Café and church is an obvious example.

Rather than building a theology of innovation from creation, we would do better to reflect on the new creation. The kingdom of God is innovation on a cosmic scale. God is dissatisfied with the existing creation. So he starts with what he's got - the world as it is - to bring about a new order, the kingdom of God. Scripture contains multiple stories that help us to make sense of this new kingdom. One of these stories is about the kingdom being like a mustard seed. The seed grows into one of the largest trees in the garden. The kingdom amplifies.

At the same time, the kingdom is always on the edge of chaos. It brings about things that are new, but these novelties are integrated into what already exists. So Revelation can talk about 'a new heaven and a new earth'. The kingdom is new, but recognisable as the universe with which we are familiar. The kingdom is not so orderly that little change occurs, nor so dramatically new that the old is completely destroyed, vanishing into chaos. The result is that our identities are transformed. We are transformed into children of God, into brothers and sisters of Christ.

Innovation happens when God's future begins to re-form the present. The result is not the obliteration of tradition. It is the transformation of tradition. The kingdom gives history new life. If you like, innovation fertilises the tradition, while tradition is the soil in which innovation grows.

Bio:

Rev'd Dr Michael Moynagh is based at Wycliffe Hall, Oxford and works for Fresh Expressions in the U.K. He is author of *Church in Life. Innovation, Mission and Ecclesiology*, London: SCM, 2017.

The old must be revealed as inadequate before the new is born. This is a challenge to leaders who believe that the main task of management is to keep everyone happy. If you want improvement, you need some people not to be happy.

Michael Moynagh

some
still point:
future
present
contemplative

ian adams

Ian Adams

Around us our world stumbles, lurches and swirls.
Seemingly beyond reason, chaotic, and fearful.
Instability is normal. Everything good is threatened.
Only darkness to come.

But a better future is possible.
A more peaceful, just and hopeful world.
The deep and forever dream of the Judaeo-Christian tradition.

Our natural instinct is to do something
to bring about the better future.
To act. To make change happen. And action, of course, matters.
But something needs to precede it.

We need to change.

The beautiful future has to take shape first within us.
Here and now. In this fragile present.
Within you and within me.

Brutality all
around; softening begins
here, pebbles rolled smooth.[1]

Only our peace will produce a peaceful world.
Or our anxiety will produce an anxious world,
our fear a fearful world,
our anger an angry world.

Ian Adams

Before we act, we need to rediscover our peace,
found in a renewed sense of our belovedness;
the bright field, some still point, from which it will be possible
to engage with the world and help to reshape it for good.

Find your still point, dawn
of your belovedness; now
rise into new day.[2]

This task will require our deep attention.
It's a way of life that needs to be practised, learned, absorbed.
A process through which we discover our belonging in God.
So that peace goes from something we long for,
and occasionally find, to who we are.

**This is the contemplative path,
and it has always been a quiet and vital (if often neglected) presence
at the heart of Christian life and mission.**

And after he had dismissed the crowds, Jesus went up the mountain by
himself to pray. When evening came, he was there alone.
Matthew 14.23

**The contemplative path always begins in some practice of stillness.
A stillness that becomes prayer,
opening up the possibility of divine encounter.**

Ian Adams

**The tradition's experience is that most of the time
this path is unspectacular.
Some seasons it can be very dark.
Occasionally, sublime.**

**But always a gift.
Revealing that we are beloved,
and deeply connected to everyone, to everything, to God.
With an energy that propels us out
with love and presence
into our world.**

When you gain interior silence you can carry it with you in the world
and pray everywhere.
Thomas Merton

Stillness becomes the source from which action
becomes possible and fruitful;
stillness the quiet spark of contemplation
lighting the fires of action.

Want to reshape the future for good?
Let's nurture a practice of stillness and prayer.
Allow that to deepen our love for God and for neighbour.
And to inspire our action.

So in God's grace
the beautiful future takes shape here and now,
with you and with me, in this fragile present,
today, every day.

Ian Adams

Resist the urge to
throw rocks or hurl boulders: skim
stones. Your peace brings change.[3]

Images:

The images for this piece were all made by Ian in winter, spring and summer of 2017 and feature the artwork *Daze IV* by Antony Gormley, on the Sidgwick Site at the University of Cambridge.

Bio:

Ian Adams works with words and images to explore the possibility of faith, hope and love reshaping the world. He is Spirituality Adviser to Church Mission Society, Tutor in Pioneering at Ridley Hall Cambridge, and partner in the Beloved Life project. He loves jazz.

Ian Adams

Endnotes:

1 Ian Adams *Unfurling* Canterbury Press 2015
2 Ian Adams *Unfurling* Canterbury Press 2015
3 Ian Adams *Unfurling* Canterbury Press 2015

opening our imprisoned imaginations: incarceration and a politics of love

max harris

>>In a recent book, I've argued that our politics has become drained of values. Politics has become technocratic - seen as the preserve of experts, regarded as a matter of engineering - and that has obscured value judgments.[1] At the same time, there has been a surge of self-interest and selfishness in societies the world over since the 1970s and 1980s, in part because of neoliberal economic reforms.

That surge has made it more difficult to speak of shared values. As well, there has been a general loss of a sense of direction in politics. Nostalgia - talk of making America great again, or references to 'Empire 2.0' in the United Kingdom in the aftermath of Brexit - has been a substitute for that sense of direction. And in that drift away from a political destination, values have also become lost.

I argue that we need to centre values in our politics again. We need those engaged in politics to be motivated by values, to embody values in the work they do, and to secure values in outcome. Values connect to the heart as well as the head. Values have a long history of being the basis for decision-making in many traditions, including in indigenous communities, religious institutions, and elsewhere.

And it's not just any values that we need to centre. In my view, the values of care, community, and creativity are particularly lacking in our politics. These three 'Cs' might form the basis for a new approach to politics – and this new approach might be underpinned by another value that we're even more timid about in political settings: the value of love. We might sum up this new approach to politics by calling it 'a politics of love'.

I made this argument in relation to the politics of New Zealand – the country I grew up in, and where I've lived for most of my life. But it is possible that the argument has broader application, to other societies: in particular the United Kingdom, and possibly beyond. The United Kingdom has seen a shifting of norms, a new common sense, in the aftermath of Thatcher's reforms of the 1980s – which has challenged collective institutions and the very idea of society as a shared endeavor. Tony Blair's government embedded a technocratic approach, especially in its reliance on the language of "what works" – a beguiling phrase that obfuscated value judgments by implying that we can arrive at a value-free judgment about what it means for a policy to "work". And there is also, at least until recently, a loss of a sense of direction in British politics: a failure to articulate the end-goal of political activity. Arguably the United Kingdom, too, needs a return to the values of care, community, and creativity – as well as a politics of love.

This chapter applies the framework of a values-based politics to one specific policy area: prisons and penal policy. The first part of the chapter explains what is wrong with prisons, in general terms, from a values-based perspective. The second part provides a brief overview of the Norwegian approach to incarceration, based on a research trip I made to Norway in late 2015. In closing, I offer some reflections about what is to be done to take a values-based approach forward, especially in the sphere of prison policy.

It is necessary at the outset to offer some caveats and conceptual clarification. Because the discussion of prisons is pitched at a level of generality, some developments related to mass incarceration around the world are not touched on: there is little discussion in what follows, for example, about the use of prisons to detain migrants (a subject that is worthy of further investigation).

By politics I mean not simply electoral politics, but the way that ideas, individuals, institutions, and identities acquire or lose power. Electoral politics is one force that affects struggles for power, but it is not the only part of politics, properly construed. Campaigns, activism, and money are all further forces in that struggle for power.

What do I mean by care, community, creativity, and love? Care refers to a deep concern for others and the environment. Community involves a recognition that we are interdependent. Creativity is about play, imagination, and producing things. I regard love as a deep sense of warmth directed towards another. A politics of love, a concept I first developed with writer Philip McKibbin[2], is simply a politics in which those engaged with politics are motivated by love, embody love in what they do, and secure love in outcome.

I do not have the same background in theology as many of the authors in this collection, and I claim no expertise in theology or spirituality. I write this chapter from the perspective of a person with a deep interest in spirituality – and I acknowledge the continuities and intersections between a values-based politics and many forms of spirituality.

What's Wrong with Prisons?

First, prisons restrict social contact. They are institutions of enforced solitude, designed for individuals who, like all of us, generally desire social interaction. Prisoners can only interact with other prisoners, guards and prison officials; in Aotearoa New Zealand, where I am from, prisoners are also entitled to one 30-minute visit a week at minimum (any further visits must be approved by individual prisons).[3]

Second, prisons suggest that prisoners are a subspecies of humanity. Prisons are separated from communities; in this way, '[t]he prisoner is detached from society ... [and] leaves it', in the words of one writer.[4] Criminologist Nicola Lacey and psychologist Hanna Pickard have observed that prisoners are made to be seen as 'out-group members in society', which also harms reintegration.[5]

Third, prisons are structurally ill-equipped to deliver rehabilitation. Although prisons are often described as correctional institutions, achieving 'corrections' in the lives of prisoners is difficult when prisoners are only surrounded by other prisoners. One ex-prisoner recently described prisons as 'a finishing school for any upcoming [sic] prisoner'; the New Zealand Principal Youth Court Judge Andrew Becroft has called prisons 'universities of crime'.[6] 'Redemption scripts' are important for prisoners to change – and these scripts are hard to write when individuals are identified every day in prison primarily as criminals.[7]

As well, prisons are not similar to the outside world, and are therefore not conducive to rehabilitation. Indeed, they are designed to be different from the outside world in, for example, how much exercise and freedom of movement is allowed, how much social interaction and visiting is allowed, and the other deprivations of physical liberty faced by prisoners. And if rehabilitation cannot be secured through prisons, then prisons are not enhancing the cause of public safety, and leave society just as vulnerable (if not more vulnerable) when individuals are released from prison.

Fourth, prisons exclude from public view a country's most serious social problems. This might have the effect of delaying any real attempts to resolve those problems. The point is well expressed by prison abolitionist and writer Angela Davis: 'Prison relieves us of the responsibility of seriously engaging with the problems of our society, especially those produced by racism and, increasingly, global capitalism.'[8]

Prisons relieve us of the responsibility of engaging with the ongoing effects of white supremacy, mental health problems and drug abuse, among other problems. It has been estimated (according to 2010 figures) that, of New Zealand's approximately 8,500 prisoners, 89 per cent have been substance abusers at some point in their lives; 60 per cent of prisoners have a personality disorder; 52 per cent have experienced anxiety or psychotic disorders; 64 per cent of male prisoners and 54 per cent of female prisoners have suffered a head injury.[9] 90 per cent of prisoners 'cannot read or write properly'.[10] It is therefore, sadly, no surprise that prisoners are 11 times more likely than the general population to commit suicide.[11]

Fifth, all around the world, prisons are ciphers for racial prejudices, with ethnic minorities invariably disproportionately represented in prison musters. In Aotearoa New Zealand, while Māori make up 15 per cent of the general population, they comprise 50.7 per cent of the prison population. In 2011, 704 out of 100,000 Māori were imprisoned;[12] this exceeds the national imprisonment rate of the US (698 per 100,000), which has the highest country-level imprisonment rate in the developed world. Such huge over-representation of Māori, which successive governments have not addressed, is partly due to the fact that – because of colonial policies of geographical dislocation, land confiscation and cultural disconnection, and the ongoing trauma of colonisation – many Māori fall into the most deprived categories of the New Zealand population, and are therefore more likely to commit crime.

But other factors are at work. A 2009 report showed that 52 per cent of convicted offenders are reconvicted within five years. Māori are more likely than Pākehā to be reimprisoned after reoffending within five years: 58 per cent of Māori are reimprisoned, as opposed to 47.3 per cent of Pākehā.[13] Given that Māori have no genetic reason to reoffend, it can only be the case that there is some form of prejudice in play that makes police or judges or others more likely to re-imprison Māori than non-Māori; indeed, Police Commissioner Mike Bush admitted the existence of unconscious bias towards Māori within the police force in 2015.[14] A similar story can be told of the over-representation of black British individuals in prison, or the over-representation of African-Americans in US prisons. While imprisonment is not the basis of racism itself, it is a particularly insidious theatre in which racist judgments are made.

Sixth, prisons are expensive. It costs $97,090 a year for a person to be incarcerated in New Zealand – far more than it costs to fund fully a year of university education for that person, or to pay them a well-salaried job.[15] When countries already have limited resources to invest in education, healthcare, housing and the future of their populations, and when prison undermines wellbeing in the ways described above, this appears to be a questionable investment.

The investment might be justified if prisons fulfilled their aims, but the seventh and final problem with prisons is that they do not achieve their purported goals. As warehouses for human beings, they do, by dint of existing, cabin some people away from the rest of the community; they are successful, to some extent, in achieving incapacitation of offenders. But evidence shows that it is not imprisonment, but likelihood of apprehension, that deters crime – so imprisonment does not serve a deterrent function, either in a general or a specific sense.[16] It is therefore those who champion deterrence through imprisonment who are out of touch – rather than those who oppose high rates of imprisonment – when they assume that crime happens through rational, methodical decision-making.

Prisons cannot be conducive environments for rehabilitation, for reasons mentioned above. Prisons might serve some public disapproval function, but it is not clear why denunciation cannot be achieved in other forms (through court judgments and more personalised processes that allow offenders to see the harm that they have done). Prisons may give us a false sense of security. But they do not contribute meaningfully towards the society that we all want, a society with as little harmful offending as possible. Instead, prisons represent a vengeful attempt by the State to punish – that is, to impose pain on – offenders.

It might be accepted that prisons are harmful, but perhaps, some might say, they are a necessary evil. Offenders deserve punishment, it could be said, for the wrongs they have committed. Victims need the closure secured by imprisonment. Some individuals – people who have committed violent crimes or repeated sex offences, for instance – need to be protected from society and from themselves. And, after all, what are the alternatives?

Each of these arguments deserves consideration, but none overwhelms the powerful case about the harms caused by prison. On what prisoners deserve: it is true that some individuals have carried out horrific acts that require a public response and accountability. But it is not clear, as Kim Workman has said, that prisons – and the experience of solitude faced by many prisoners – do hold prisoners to account. Moreover, what is a 'fitting' or 'proportionate' response to a crime has changed over time, and prisons have only been seen as the dominant approach to serious crime since the early 1800s, when prison systems were established in the US and elsewhere.[17]

The claim that victims require closure through imprisonment also makes intuitive sense but needs to be investigated further. While we should be careful about generalising about the needs of all victims (which is part of the problem of fixing a link between victim closure and prisons), in many cases victims or survivors want to be assured of their safety and to avoid retraumatisation. Prison may sometimes provide the best assurance of a victim's safety – but it also might result in retraumatisation, including when the prisoner is inevitably released. A more direct strategy for addressing victims' needs is to provide State-funded counselling and support for victim trauma following crime. In all of this we should remember that, although victims' voices need to be heard and respected, the court system also exists in order to determine the appropriate response to crime, a step removed from the perpetrator and victim (if there is a victim in the case), following the trauma of a crime.

Third, in relation to the protection of individuals and society, some people do indeed have deep pathologies and problems that make it possible that they will commit multiple offences over the course of a lifetime.[18] Some individuals committing violent crime seem to fit this description, as do many who commit sexual offences. Prisons that remove these individuals from society appear to offer the protection that society – and these individuals – need. However, it has already been noted above that because prisons are artificial environments, with limited social contact, prisoners may leave at least as likely to commit crime (and perhaps more likely) as when they entered. Prison does provide temporary protection. But we need to think harder, and work harder, as a society if we are to be truly committed to a society where there is no harmful offending.

Finally, it is simply wrong to assert that there are no alternatives to imprisonment: it is merely the case that alternatives to imprisonment require more imagination (or creativity, to recall a progressive value). There are already a number of effective alternatives to short-term imprisonment in place around the world, including police-level diversion, electronic monitoring, home detention and restorative justice. Some of these alternatives have limitations, but they reveal that other policy options do exist. As for alternatives to long-term imprisonment, other countries – in particular, those in Scandinavia – have developed a number. Below I discuss in more detail what Norway has done in this field, based on a research trip I made there in late 2015. This again demonstrates that to say that there are no alternatives to imprisonment is a stretch at best.

Stepping back, and returning to the touchstones of care, community, creativity, and love: it can also be said that prisons fail the test of upholding our fundamental values. Prisons embody a denial of care, in particular in the way that they deny social contact to individuals. They represent a distortion of the value of the community, in that they attempt to cordon off inmates as non-members of our community. And they are inconsistent with creativity; indeed, prisons are a failure of imagination – they are a lazy, sloppy response to the challenges thrown up by wrongdoing in any society. They are, in short, the antithesis of a politics of love.

What this section highlights, I hope, is that prisons should not be maintained in their current form if we are committed to values of community, care and creativity. Something must be done. But what? And how?

A useful frame for moving away from prisons in their current form what Angela Davis calls 'decarceration'.[19] Decarceration is about radically reversing the creep of mass incarceration. It is not about immediately emptying our prisons; it is rather about a phased departure from a reliance on incarceration as a response to wrongdoing.[20] Decarceration involves finding particular leverage points to target in order to reduce incarceration, and it can be supplemented by positive policy approaches that substitute for failed carceral practices.[21]

The Norwegian Approach

Norway's approach to criminal justice has been widely applauded. Norway incarcerates people at a rate of 74 per 100,000, one of the lowest figures in the world. Norwegian prisons are known for being humane. As well, Norway has advanced victim support, including State compensation for victims of crime. With the financial support of the New Zealand Law Foundation, I travelled to Norway in late 2015 to explore how it has built this criminal justice system. I spoke off-the-record with a judge and a policeman, and had conversations with a criminal defence lawyer, a women's rights legal NGO, a legal academic and others (including many young people).

I had made inquiries about trying to visit a prison while in Norway, but with little luck. Then, after sending a message to a generic Norwegian public sector email address, I received a phone call out of the blue while I sat at a computer in downtown Oslo. A kind employee of the Norwegian Correctional Services Department, Ellen Bjercke, introduced herself. The good news, she told me, was that I would be able to visit a prison in Norway during the week I was there: Bastøy Prison. The bad news? It was a few hours away, and would require a long car trip and a ferry ride. Just as I began to worry about whether the journey was possible, though – in an act of extraordinary trust and kindness – Bjercke said she'd be happy to drive me.

A few days later, I met Ellen Bjercke on the Oslo waterfront early in the morning, and she drove me to the Bastøy ferry, cheerfully telling me en route about her experiences of the criminal justice system. When she dropped me off, she told me that the ferry was managed and operated by inmates at Bastøy Prison – one sign of the prison's thoughtful approach to developing skills in its inmates. I spoke a little to the inmates who worked as crew on the ferry, and a few minutes later, I arrived at Bastøy. It used to be called Devil's Island, because it was home to a notoriously grim boys' home. But since the 1980s the island has changed significantly, and it's now the site of an open prison, a place of wide paths, green lawns and tall trees.

In a small room, I was briefed by Tom Eberhardt, the Bastøy governor. Not a tall man, Eberhardt looked tough but friendly. He told me and several other visitors that Bastøy has a high staff-inmate ratio: 72 staff for 115 inmates (with 20–25 of the inmates being foreign nationals). There is a long waiting list for inmates wanting to transfer there. And inmates there have a choice of working in agriculture (in fields, forest or with animals), maintenance and buildings, on the ferry, in the prison's kitchen, in the library, in carpentry, or on labour and welfare issues. One of the inmates was studying for a PhD in criminology. Twenty to thirty per cent of the prison's food is grown on the island, and working with animals is seen as a way to teach inmates empathy. I took a walk around later to see the housing on the island and to have lunch. The inmates live in flats of different sizes. Inmates are placed carefully in flats to teach skills: inmates with reduced hygiene or social skills are placed alongside inmates known to have greater abilities in these areas.

Tom Eberhardt explained a little bit of the philosophy that underpins the prison's operation. A key tenet is 'the principle of normality', he said, 'Everyday life in prison isn't meant to be different from everyday life outside of prison.' 'Inmates behave,' Eberhardt added, 'because they actually like being here'. Another principle is 'creating good neighbours': the prison aims to highlight that inmates are dependent on others, and that they need to be sensitive to the needs of others. When released, inmates 'will have to deal with other people's mindsets', he noted, so why not prepare inmates for this interaction within a community while in prison? He also observed, 'If you treat people badly, they will become bitter, angry – not be a good neighbor.' Helping inmates to become good neighbours therefore requires the prison to treat the inmates well. Bastøy is a 'human ecological prison', too, based on the idea that we can take 'responsibility for ourselves by taking care of nature'. Care was clearly central to Bastøy's functioning: if you have no care for nature, Eberhardt said, you can't take care of yourselves.

Bastøy is clearly a successful prison, and the Norwegian Correctional Services Department – and Tom Eberhardt – are justifiably proud of it. There has been no violent episode there for the past 30 years. The prison helps to reintegrate its inmates into society. Eberhardt attributed this to the fact that '[t]hey're not released with hatred towards society'. As well, he told me, 'We haven't taken their hope away.' Eberhardt rejected the idea that justice should be about revenge. That cold day in December, he looked me in the eye and said: 'Revenge [in criminal justice] is like pissing your pants in Norway. It feels good. But then you start to freeze.'

How has Norway developed a criminal justice system with prisons such as Bastøy? Eberhardt: 'The culture in Norway is a forgiving culture.' In addition, he discussed the role of empathy, saying that policy-makers in Norway have asked,

'What kind of prison facility [would] you want for your son?' The point about empathy was echoed by Kari Henriksen, a Norwegian Labour MP with a deep interest in criminal justice, who told me that she could imagine herself being violent or becoming a criminal, and that such empathy was essential to policy-making. I cannot imagine a politician in the United Kingdom, or New Zealand, being brave enough to say the same.

After returning to Oslo, I met with four representatives of KROM (the Norwegian Association of Penal Reform) to explore further the reasons for Norway's distinctive approach to criminal justice: Thomas Mathiesen, Ole Kristian Hjemdal, Sturla Falck and Kristian Andenaes. Thomas Mathiesen is a well-known Norwegian criminologist now in his 80s, the author of books such as *The Politics of Abolition* and *Prison on Trial*. Hjemdal, Falck and Andenaes have all done academic research and practical work in the criminal justice system. All four of them welcomed me warmly in a meeting room in an office block in downtown Oslo, and chatted for around two hours about their experiences and impressions.

Norway has not always been progressive in its criminal justice policy, they underscored. Key changes were made in the 1970s, and Mathiesen, Hjemdal, Falck, and Andenaes emphasised three factors as being central to these shifts. First, the climate of the 1960s and 1970s was important. "We are children of our time," one said. 1968 was a year of protest, especially in Europe, and the decade also brought a sense of hope and imagination to political debates. Criminal justice reforms in Norway were hence 'part of a larger change of values and basic policies'.

A second factor was the work of the Norwegian Labour Party politician Inger Louise Valle. Valle pushed hard, they told me, to introduce legislative changes in the criminal justice field that had a far-reaching effect on Norway's low prison population.

Third, I heard about the 'long-term insistence' of groups like KROM, campaigning to entrench a greater spirit of forgiveness in Norwegian society. The KROM representatives were reluctant to give themselves too much credit. But it was clear, from this conversation and the off-the-record remarks of others, that KROM had made a significant difference: including through its almost fifty-year history of annual conferences bringing together inmates, the public sector, lawyers, academics, students and judges. In sum, then: empathy (not far removed from the value of care), a broader climate of progressive values, individual political leadership, and persistent campaigning were identified as the main reasons for why Norway's criminal justice system has become humane, forgiving – and largely effective.

Such was the perspective of one set of observers. Mathiesen, Hjemdal, Falck and Andenaes were at pains not to romanticise Norway, and they highlighted the return of punitive incarceration policies in recent years. Nevertheless, their insights – and my visit to Bastøy Prison – provided some hints about how a country can build a justice system that is based on more than just revenge.

What Can Be Done?

What, then, can be done in places such as the United Kingdom to initiate a process of decarceration? The Norwegian example offers some lessons. To the extent that prisons need to remain, they can be redesigned according to principles of 'normality' and 'creating good neighbours'. Protective institutions, redesigned along these lines, should have high staff-inmate ratios, options for meaningful (and properly remunerated) work, and support for education and skill acquisition.

But there are also specific policy ideas that can be borrowed from elsewhere to reduce the size of prison populations. Greater use of restorative justice in place of short-term sentences (as is used in the New Zealand youth justice system), stronger funding for problem-solving courts such as drug courts (which offer supervised rehabilitation), legislation directing judges to consider the effects of colonisation on indigenous offenders in countries with indigenous populations (of the kind that exists in Canada), and investments in rehabilitation are all practical steps that can be taken. Sometimes a contrast is drawn between prison 'reform' and prison 'abolition', but there need not be a tension between the approaches: if a series of specific steps add up to transformative change, an abolitionist goal can be pursued through particular reforms.

The more fundamental challenge, however, beyond listing useful policies is to enact the foundational values shift that would make it easier for politicians to pass the legislative changes described above. How can political values shift towards the values I described at the outset of this chapter – values such as care, community, creativity, and love? My view is that it will require a combination of top-down leadership and bottom-up pressure. A new generation of politicians is needed, motivated by these values and informed by a broad set of life experiences. But collective action, driven by values, is needed to put pressure on these politicians.

The responsibility lies with all of us, to use whatever skills and resources we have to take this project forward – whether these are financial or intellectual or practical otherwise. It will take all of the expertise, all of the imagination, and all of the love we can muster.

So what are we waiting for?

Bio:

Max Harris is an Examination Fellow in Law at All Souls College, Oxford. He is author of the book, *The New Zealand Project,* and his public writing has appeared in a range of outlets, including *Aeon, The Pantograph Punch, PopMatters*, and *The Conversation.* He has also worked in a range of campaigns, including with the groups JustSpeak and Generation Zero in New Zealand and Rhodes Must Fall in Oxford.

Endnotes:

1. The book is called *The New Zealand Project* (Bridget Williams Books, Wellington, 2017). This chapter draws on parts of Chapter Seven of *The New Zealand Project.* I am grateful to Bridget Williams Books for permission to reproduce excerpts from that chapter.

2. See Max Harris and Philip McKibbin, 'The Politics of Love', *The Aotearoa Project*, 20 May 2015, available online at https://theaotearoaproject.wordpress.com/2015/05/20/the-politics-of-love-max-harris-and-philip-mckibbin/ (last accessed 14 September 2017).

3. See JustSpeak, *Unlocking Prisons: How We Can Improve New Zealand's Prison System* (2014, Rimutaka Prison Printing Press), p. 63.

4. Michel Foucault, *Discipline and Punish* (Vintage Books, 1975), p. 110.

5. Nicola Lacey and Hanna Pickard, 'To Blame or To Forgive? Reconciling Punishment and Forgiveness in Criminal Justice' (2015) *Oxford Journal of Legal Studies*, p. 23.

6. See JustSpeak, *Unlocking Prisons*, above n 1, at p. 60; Andrew Becroft used the phrase 'universities of crime' at several public talks in 2009–2011, and the phrase appears in Judge Andrew Becroft, 'How to Turn a Child Offender into an Adult Criminal: Ten Easy Steps', Children and the Law International Conference, 7 September 2009.

7. See Shadd Maruna, *Making Good: How Ex-Convicts Reform and Rebuild their Lives* (American Psychological Association, 2001).

8. Angela Y. Davis, *Are Prisons Obsolete?* (Seven Stories Press, 2003), p. 16.

9. JustSpeak, *Unlocking Prisons*, above n 5, pp. 63–64.

10. Ibid, at p. 67.

11. Ibid, at p. 64.

12. Synod Prison Task Group, *Incarceration in New Zealand* (2011), p. 2.

13. JustSpeak, *Unlocking Prisons*, above n 5, at p. 55.

14. Harata Brown, 'Police Working on Unconscious Bias towards Māori', Māori Television, 29 November 2015, available online at https://www.maoritelevision.com/news/national/police-working-on-unconscious-bias-towards-maori (last accessed 11 January 2017). My thanks to a Bridget Williams Books reader for drawing this to my attention.

15. Ibid, at p. 7.

16. Ibid, at pp. 17–21.

17. On how what is 'fitting' and 'proportionate' can change over time and across context, see: Lacey and Pickard, 'To Blame or To Forgive? Reconciling Punishment and Forgiveness in Criminal Justice', above n 12.

18. Often this is described in terms of 'risk' or 'dangerousness'. These terms have little or no scientific basis.

19. See Angela Y. Davis, *Are Prisons Obsolete?* (Seven Stories Press, 2003).

20. Chase Madar, *Hard Time: Two Books Exploring the Roots of the Criminal-Justice Crisis*, BookForum, Sept/Oct/Nov 2017, available online at http://www.bookforum.com/inprint/024_03/18449 (last accessed 13 September 2017).

21. There is useful analysis of this approach in: Allegra M. McLeod, 'Prison Abolition and Grounded Justice' (2015) 62 *UCLA Law Review* 1156–1239 at pp. 1161–1172.

Prisons are inconsistent with creativity; indeed, prisons are a failure of imagination – they are a

lazy, sloppy response to
the challenges thrown
up by wrongdoing in
any society. They are, in
short, the antithesis of a
politics of love.

Max Harris

open house: reimagining church spaces

steve collins

>>All spaces communicate values.

This isn't just a matter of surface style. Physical arrangements themselves enable or disable particular power structures, behaviours and relationships. When our needs are at odds with our surroundings, we find ourselves subtly opposed - the rooms aren't the right size, the furniture is awkward, our hospitality is undermined, our rituals are cramped.

Environments don't stand still, because culture and society change, so it's no surprise that most Christian communities struggle with the spaces they have inherited. We are camping out in other people's theological and liturgical arrangements, like tenants in a rented house. At similar moments in the past, Christian communities have not been afraid to radically alter their surroundings to suit their changed needs.

The ideas shown here are not meant to be final, or exhaustive, or mutually exclusive solutions. They demonstrate possibilities, for other spatial orderings and therefore other ways of being the people of God. They are an attempt to step out of the usual arguments about pews and kneelers and organs - where we have already limited ourselves to tinkering with what we inherited.

Instead this asks - what arrangements would really serve us and our wider communities in the 21st century? What kinds of space would really support our wholeness and flourishing? If we can begin to imagine those spaces, we can begin to work out how to get there.

Perhaps it will be difficult and expensive - previous generations made great sacrifices and we still live off their investment in the future. But it may also be easier and cheaper than we think, if we can identify small key changes that will really make a difference to how our buildings work and feel. It's easy to be paralysed by the large things that we cannot do, when there may be a succession of small things that we *can* do, if we know where we are going.

1300: church as throne room

big idea: **adoration**

the setting: **images and altars**

carrier of meaning: **rituals**

how we take part: **watching**

primary activity:
short devotional acts

theological model: **god as king**

1700: church as school room

big idea: **education**

the setting: **pulpit and pews**

carrier of meaning: **words**

how we take part: **listening**

primary activity:
long teaching sessions

theological model: **god as lawyer**

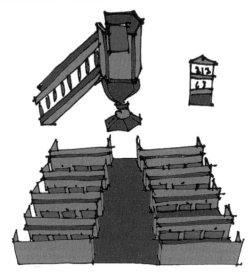

2017: most of our spaces are

2100: church as living room

big idea: **interaction**

the setting: **chairs and tables**

carrier of meaning: **stories**

how we take part: **sharing**

primary activity:
social networking

theological model: **god as host**

Steve Collins

different kinds of church space:

moving from

church as an event
in spaces that are unused
the rest of the time

to

church as an environment
in which events can happen

1: the big table

big wide wooden tables[1], 10-20-30 people each side
meeting making eating working
what's on the table for you to play with or pray with?
who will you sit next to?
what do you bring to the table?

2: meditate/relax

rugs, floor cushions, small stools and tables, couches
tall candles (so that they're above your head when you lie down)
ambient music, sound art, guided meditations
look at the beautiful ceiling[2], relax, be silent, switch off

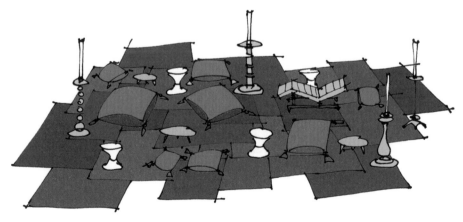

3: living room

small conversational groups
high backed sofas[3] for acoustic and visual privacy
discussion, prayer, counselling
be with friends

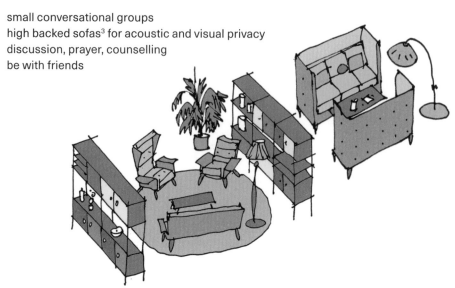

4: library

knowledge and assistance space - information, study, social services[4]
self directed and with helpers
2-person workstations, bookstacks, printers
small pods for private meetings

5: theatre

larger numbers of people with a central focus[5]
a space to share and show
danger! do not use as default church space

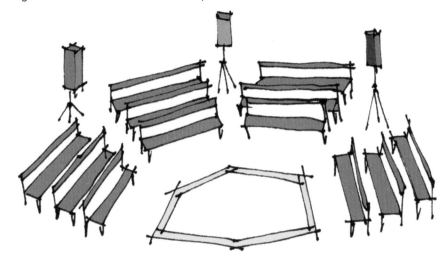

6: factory

small scale / artisan production
locally sourced ingredients, local distribution
giving employment, teaching skills
part of the local economy, sustainable

7: kitchen

cheap good food for all from local sourced ingredients
a social place, a hub for the neighborhood
offers training and employment

8: asset space

lettable space for small businesses and startups
a mix of shared facilities and private areas
an income generator and seedbed for social enterprise

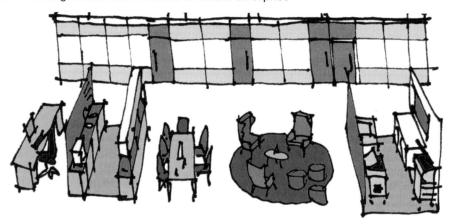

what does your space sound like?

for **conversation** - light jazz, chill out, melodic pop

for **meditation, prayer** - numinous, mystical, sound art

communal singing belongs in the theatre space
make it a big thing, not an interruption to something else

avoid dominating and emotional forms
unless you want to take a specific group on a specific journey

consider the **musical story** of your community
and others that you want to feel comfortable in your space

beware of 'religious' music - it reinforces stereotypes
of how people feel and behave in churches

how is the space lit?

what **atmosphere** do you want to create?
how do you want to **feel**?

what do you want to **highlight**?
what do you want to **hide**?

floor lamps and **table lamps** for **pools of light**
decorative lights as points of interest

if people need to **read**, try to **provide light close to them**
rather than making everywhere bright

variety is always better than uniformity

food and drink:

part of the scenario for the big table, living room and kitchen available in the background for the other spaces

eucharist:

is **easiest** around the big table, and in the theatre
is **beautiful** in the meditation space
is **hard** to get everyone together in the living room
is **not appropriate** in the library and factory

duration:

these environments (except for the theatre space) are
not tied to events of fixed duration

they run **continously**

they are **not temporary**
no return to pews for the sunday service[6]

for a different experience **go to a different space**

key operating principles:

hospitality
I feel welcome and comfortable in here

availability
it's there whenever I need it

openness
any kind of person can use it

church spaces as **resources**
for the surrounding community

ourselves as **hosts,
assistants and enablers**

the **living spaces** of the people of god
open to the public and the community

the present situation:

since **one church building** serves **one christian community,**
either:

one building has to do **everything**
therefore **many scene changes** are required

or

one use is dominant in the space
and therefore **dominates the life of the community**

(right now it's mostly a mashup of throneroom and schoolroom)

but **general purpose space** (the 'school hall' approach)
means that **utility and durability** take precedence

tight budgets mean that everything is **cheap**

there is an assumption that users will take **no care**

plastic chairs
fluorescent lights
drab carpets
bland colours
warning notices
infrequent maintenance

this is **defensive not welcoming**

present: church as retail chain

the legacy of denominational competition

every place has a lot of churches

parallel clones, **competing** for custom

very similar offerings except for liturgical details

each claims to be a 'one-stop shop'
for all your needs

every village has one branch of each 'chain'

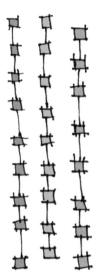

future: church as network

if we could drop the denominational boundaries

all those churches could become one resource

diverse and complementary

very different offerings to meet all kinds of
spiritual and social needs

cooperation and support for other ministries

every village has one of each kind of space

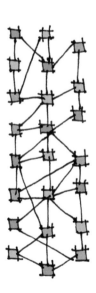

from:
each building trying to offer everything in **competition** with others

to:
each building as a particular offering **complementary** to others

what are the good qualities of your building?

ambience, beauty, heritage, facilities, location?
stained glass, good kitchen, on the high street?

what are the bad qualities of your building?

toilets, seats, layout, notices?
poor heating, instant coffee, musty smell?

what key changes would make a big difference?

small things can have a big impact on how a space feels
and how people feel about a space

what does hospitality look and feel like?

what are you **welcoming** people to?
what can your space do **best**?
what is the local **need**?

missional communities create servant spaces

1300: throne room

adoration
images and altars
rituals
watching
short devotional acts
god as **king**

1700: school room

education
pulpit and pews
words
listening
long teaching sessions
god as **lawyer**

2100: living room

interaction
chairs and tables
stories
sharing
social networking
god as **host**

Bio:

Steve Collins is an architect specialising in workplace design for corporate clients in the financial, technology and legal sectors. He is a member of Grace church community www.freshworship.org, based in Ealing, west London. He is interested in the relationships between organisational power structures, technology and the physical environment.

Endnotes:

1. This form of table is open access, non-hierarchical - not a dinner party or banquet. It supports small group collaboration and individuals dropping in and out.

Two- and four-person tables, as found in a restaurant, create small inward-looking groups - private huddles in a crowded room. This doesn't seem quite right for a church gathering. Large linear tables can seat small groups, maybe several on a table, but there is always the possibility of others joining in, or the focus of attention shifting along the table. Users are more aware of the room as a whole.

How long can a table be? There is something wonderful about a really long table - but it takes a while to get to the other side!

2. Many of our buildings are very beautiful. We should spend more time looking at them, rather than at a hymnbook, piece of paper, or even projection screen. Beauty is a gift and a sign.

It feels subversive to lie around on the floor of a church, in comfort, looking at the ceiling. Clearly we have opted out of discipline and hierarchy. We have become vulnerable and open.

3. The high back sofas are very popular in offices now, for semi-private conversation or work, without cutting the occupants off from the room. They also feel cozy and sheltering.

4. Many churches are now engaged in helping people navigate the benefit system, social services, the health system, legal matters etc. Much of this is online, which is a problem for people who have little internet access or lack navigational skills. These workstations allow two people to sit together for mutual assistance. The small pods enable private counselling and discussion. Printers allow people to make records and take material away with them.

5. This arrangement avoids putting the central performers 'above' or 'at the head of' the rest.

6. One reason why alternative church arrangements struggle is lack of availability. They exist for a short while and then are replaced by the usual setup. You might never know they existed, or you might never be able to attend at the right time.

And the set-up and removal adds a lot of work for groups or churches who are already dealing with the difficulty of doing other kinds of things differently. If the new arrangements can stay in place we might be able to develop convincing new forms of life and activity.

how to...
cope with
disabled
dreams

emma major

>>I'm a pioneer minister and feel most comfortable in the places less commonly inhabited by most ministers, walking alongside people as they dream of how their lives might be and introducing them to God as we journey. Over the last five years this has included crying with families whose babies have died, supporting women coping with post-natal depression, providing space for young mothers and their toddlers, creating new forms of church including messy, café and forest churches and forming a missional community. Right now, I am developing an online prayer and discipling network for disabled people who, like me, have found themselves struggling to access society and church.

Each of these communities started as a dream; an idea planted by God in the situation I found myself. They have evolved through experience and drawn on the gifts and skills God knew I had in my toolkit. But at the beginning they were all just an image in my mind at a time of disablement, a seed which has grown over time until, looking back, the growth through change becomes clear.

At the CMS Conversation Day in November I gave a talk entitled 'Disabled Dreams: Coping with Change'. This talk was the result of a period of reflection about my experience of dreaming with God and yet being disabled time and again, before coping with the change and dreaming once more. As I shared my experiences and presented my model for coping with change it became clear to me that the disablements themselves are all part of God's calling on my life. This 'How to' article brings together my original talk, the model for coping with change and some of my ongoing reflections.

Model for coping with change

Dream

In the words of Martin Luther King "I have a dream".

I have many dreams, aims, ideas and plans; God is good at using my creativity and showing me what He would like me to do for Him. Unfortunately, life has a habit of getting in the way of these dreams; life literally keeps disabling me. This disablement is frustrating, upsetting and often depressing. I don't like change, it brings out my inner toddler and often results in a tantrum. Luckily, once I chat with God and reconnect with adult thinking, I always find a way to cope. In fact, He has always reinvented the dream and created something better than I had previously imagined.

There have been a number of major change points in my life; I'm going through one right now as Multiple Sclerosis progresses through my body and causes mobility problems, pain and sight loss. It is this current disablement which has caused me to reflect on my dreams; what it means to be disabled; how we can cope with change as individuals, pioneers and communities and what light may shine through brokenness. But before this there were a series of miscarriages which resulted in the dream of a support group for women in similar circumstances; the development of liturgy for a service of remembrance; and the writing of books. Ten years before, intense depression left me on my knees and completely open to God; that was when I heard His call on my life. Through each disabled dream came a light of hope and a new dream. But first we have to grieve....

Grieve

Jean Vanier, founder of the 130 l'Arche communities around the world, has written about disability and theology. In *Community and Growth* he says "Growth begins when we start to accept our own weakness". Jesus healed disabilities; the blind man, the woman at the well, the dead, children and even the tax collectors. Jesus knew that this was necessary to bring them into community with others and with God. This was the love which rejoices in each and every one of us for who we are; a love which wants us to love ourselves and others despite our brokenness.

Most of us are not healed dramatically in the way that Jesus healed, but love, acceptance and companionship through grief are a blessing which can heal more than we appreciate in our fast paced, success driven society. We need to give ourselves the care and time to mourn the changes in our lives and/or ministry; to acknowledge the pain, disappointment, loss or anger and come to a place of acceptance before we move on. But to do this we need to lean...

Lean

In *Drawn into the Mystery of Jesus through the Gospel of John* Jean Vanier says "The message of this gospel is simple. It is about being chosen to become a friend of Jesus. It is about mutual presence and learning from each other. To live as Jesus lived and to love as he loved". We need to learn to lean; to reduce the value we place on standing strong and firm and instead embrace mutual dependence and the benefit of leaning on each other in times of trouble. And, of course, we can lean on God through prayer and Bible study, with communities and with spiritual directors or guides. Through this leaning we can rid ourselves of our disappointment and pain and start to listen....

Listen

In Japan, broken objects are often repaired with gold – the art is called Kintsugi. The flaw is seen as a unique piece of the object's history and adds to its beauty. Jean Vanier wrote "Sharing weakness and difficulties is more nourishing for others than sharing our successes", it is what God wants of us within communities. It is what pioneers are called to create; what I feel called to in my disabling, to allow the light to break through the brokenness of life to heal others. But more importantly I am learning to listen to the experiences of others as they have journeyed through their disabled dreams and to hear lessons through that which talk to me. Through community, as well as individually, we can hear God's still small voice as he shows us a new dream for our lives. And so we dream again.

Dreaming through change

I have always seen the disabling times in my life as problems to be solved, as hurdles to be overcome; but experience, reflection and prayer is teaching me that problems and hurdles are everywhere. It is in these times of weakness that I find God with me and see His call on my life. It is in these times that God shines light into the brokenness and seals gaps with His Gold.

God wants us to focus on the opportunities to serve Him. Life is not about merely coping with change but about leaning, trusting and embracing God's call to be disciples in communities together.

Bio:

My name: Emma Major
My location: Urban sprawl between Reading and Wokingham in Berkshire
My role: Lay Pioneer Minister at St Nicolas Earley
My mission call: Dreaming with God

Emma Major

Disabled Dreams

Dreaming of sight, dark turned to light
Dreaming of faces and familiar old spaces
Dreams they have changed, disabled again
Shadowed, obscured; but dreams still assured

Grief hits again, knocks me over in pain
Of what will not be, what I might not now see
Yet in the dark, God whispers to my heart
"Do not be afraid, I will show you the way"

"Lean now on me and see what I see
A future so clear, believe me my dear
I need you as before, perhaps even more
My call on your life continues in strife"

Listening is not easy as grief overwhelms me
But everyone I meet, reminds me to defeat
The doubt and fear, to keep hope and faith near
I lean, listen, follow; into the unknown tomorrow

We need to learn to lean; to reduce the value we place on standing strong and firm and instead embrace mutual dependence and the benefit of leaning on each other in times of trouble.

Emma Major

tarkovsky's stalker:
film, folly, and
future faith

colin heber-percy

One

>>Dogged by problems from the start, Andrei Tarkovsky's masterpiece was almost never made. Shooting was scheduled to begin at Isfara, Tadjikistan in April 1977, but these plans had to be abandoned when the area was hit by a violent earthquake.

Having relocated to Tallinn in Estonia, filming could begin. But after three months' work, Tarkovsky (1934-1986), found the rushes were poor and the film-stock degraded; furious, he blamed the suppliers, he blamed his cameraman for failing to check the quality of the film, and he blamed the technicians at his production company, Mosfilm, for using the wrong development procedures. Tarkovsky describes the situation in his diary, as a 'total disaster.' (Tarkovsky, 1994:146) But in that disaster Tarkovsky found the motivation to carry on:

[the disaster is] so conclusive that one actually has the sense of a fresh stage, a new step to be taken – and that gives one hope. (Tarkovsky, 1994:146)

This dynamic of disaster, despair, and then stepping – unexpectedly – into hope finds full and moving expression in the film he went on to make. *Stalker* is shaped and characterised by this movement, a sense of being impelled – in the face of every conceivable setback, obstacle and doubt – towards something better, something elusive, intangible, something that draws us towards the margins but which is also at the heart of ourselves. In short, *Stalker* is a film about faith.

As it is explored in *Stalker*, faith is depicted less as a defined and codified belief system and more as crisis and struggle, as demanding, dangerous, transgressive. And as such, it transforms and shapes – ruins and remodels the lives of the characters.

The film's plot is simple. Some men go off in search of something; they fail to find it; they come home. The end. *Stalker* is, in essence, a shaggy dog story, or a wild goose chase. The eponymous Stalker, an illegal guide, leaves his wife and disabled daughter in order to lead two men – a writer and a professor – on a journey to find a fabled Room in which their deepest desires will be fulfilled, or so the Stalker claims. So he believes. This Room lies hidden at the heart of an area of land – the Zone – that has been cordoned off by the military. At the beginning of the film we are presented with an ominous 'report' from a fictitious scientist, a Nobel Laureate, who describes how the Zone came into existence.

*Was it a meteorite? A visit of inhabitants from the cosmic abyss? One way or another our small country has seen the birth of a miracle – the Zone.
(Stalker, 1979)* [1]

And yet when we finally reach this place, there appears to be nothing miraculous about it at all. There is nothing extra-terrestrial or even extra-ordinary about what we see in the Zone. Just derelict buildings, tunnels, rusting tanks, sheds: ruins of the post-industrial hinterland of a port city being slowly reclaimed by natural processes, particularly by water.

Water saturates almost every scene – standing in puddles, flowing, falling, dripping, drifting, rippling in a glass, disrupted at the bottom of a well. And it pours through the vast concrete spaces and corroding silos that litter the landscape. We are led through these waters by the Stalker himself, a John the Baptist figure propelled across borders and boundaries into a wilderness, preaching repentance: a new way of being: 'Let everything that's been planned come true. Let them believe!' (*Stalker*, 1979)

But believe in what? Tarkovsky tantalises us with references to aliens and meteorites, teases us with contemporary science-fiction tropes, but fails to deliver them, leaving us wondering, wandering. Like the Stalker's companions, the Writer and the Professor, we are led through a physical landscape that stubbornly refuses to corroborate any of the Stalker's claims or warnings. And so the journey of the mismatched trio finds a psychological analogue in our own doubts, our own wavering faith in the Zone and the Stalker's reliability. To make this journey, to agree to follow this man, is to run a risk. The gospel parallel is obvious. In the context of the film, a journey into the Zone is to break the law. Many do not return. And those who do, face arrest and prison. In the film, as in the gospel, risk underpins the whole enterprise. Risk of arrest; risk of being wrong.

Two

Ubi stabilitas, ibi religio. (AS 35:353)

Where there is stability, there is religion. So said Abbot Lugidus (or Molua), the sixth century founder of the monastery of Clonfert among many others. For Lugidus, the religious life is rooted, static.[2] If we accept Lugidus's statement as normative of religious life in general then we must also accept that Tarkovsky is an avowedly irreligious filmmaker. In his own words:

The artist seeks to destroy the stability by which society lives, for the sake of drawing closer to the ideal. Society seeks stability, the artist – infinity. (Tarkovsky, 1986:192)

The artist destroys that which makes religion possible. The romantic notion of the iconoclastic and isolated artist was peculiarly potent for Tarkovsky during the tortuously difficult filming of *Stalker*. But in medieval terms, in Lugidus's terms, to live in isolation, to become unrooted from one's social context is to become a gyrovagus, a vagabond. To wander is to err, to be in error.

And yet journey lies at the heart of Christian witness from the beginning; immediately following his baptism, the Spirit drives Jesus *out* into the wilderness (Mk.1:12; Mt.4:1; Lk.4:1) just as God had driven Adam and Eve out of Paradise. The foundational narrative of the Jewish people is a wandering, a searching in the wilderness. And in his turn, Jesus commissions the apostles (literally 'the sent out'), instructing them to 'take nothing for their journey, except a mere staff - no bread, no bag, no money in their belt.' (Mk.6:7-8)

Juxtaposing the scriptural stress on searching, journeying with Lugidus's claim concerning *stabilitas* appears to reveal a real tension in the way religious life is *lived*. Is it ideally static and stable, or dynamic, risky, and unstable? This tension is manifest in *Stalker*'s structure: a stable, nuclear unit is broken; wife, daughter, and home are left, and a quixotic adventure embarked upon, then a return in failure, and to forgiveness.

It is faith that impels the men on their illicit journey into the Zone, faith in the existence of the Room, faith in the legends and stories. And as we have seen, the journey is fruitless. I suggested earlier that there is something of the shaggy dog story about the plot of this film. A shaggy dog story is a joke that takes you on a long and ultimately pointless journey, and it works by bathos, by *lacking* a punchline, by letting you down. It is *just* a journey.

In his *Life of Moses*, Gregory of Nyssa describes the journey of Moses as an endless ascent towards the perfection of God. For Gregory, this ascent is metaphorically represented in scripture by Moses' climbing Mount Sinai. He continually climbed to the step above and never ceased to rise higher, because he always found a step higher than the one he had attained. (Gregory of Nyssa, 1978:113-4)

Gregory uses landscape, as does Tarkovsky, to represent psychological terrain. The finite landscape – and Moses' journey through it – becomes an analogue for his striving towards perfection, towards God. And paradox inevitably lies at the heart of this analogue because landscape is limited, determinate, whereas God, that towards which Moses is striving, is limitless and absolutely undetermined; the journey must be endless, and therefore – in a sense – fruitless. There can be no punchline.

The true vision of God consists... in this, that the soul that looks up to God never ceases to desire him. Moses' desire is filled by the very fact that it remains unfulfilled. (Gregory of Nyssa, 1979:55)

Gregory is fascinated by God's saying to Moses, 'Here is a place beside me.' (Ex.33.21) How, Gregory wonders, can there be a place *beside* the placeless? 'For to something unquantitative (God) there is no measure.' (Gregory of Nyssa, 1978:242)

Gregory's solution to the dilemma lies in a spiritual, analogical reading of the Exodus text: the mountain is to be read as a symbol of the unlimited and infinite. He has God say the following to Moses:

Your desire for what is still to come has expanded and you have not reached satisfaction in your progress and whereas you do not see any limit to the Good, but your yearning always looks for more, the *place with me* is so great that the one running in it is never able to cease from his progress. (Gregory of Nyssa, 1978:242; my italics)

Gregory returns to this theme in his commentary on the Song of Songs; it is our duty, he states there, 'always to rise up, drawing nearer and nearer along the way, and never ceasing.' (Gregory of Nyssa, PG44:876C).[3] The 'place with me' is categorically not within the walls of the monastery, it is not *stabilitas*; it is the infinity which Tarkovsky's artist seeks. I suggest this dynamic 'place with me' through which we are called to run and never cease from running finds a modern analogical articulation in Tarkovsky's Zone – a hallowed place, a place that elicits yearning, that ultimately withholds satisfaction, and that appears to demand some form of metanoia, a moral commitment.

In recent years there has been a renewed emphasis on the language of journey in relation to faith. The tendency has been to see this journey as having religious faith as the destination; it is a journey *to* faith. In *Stalker*, as in Gregory of Nyssa, the notion of 'journey' is importantly different. Here it is the journey itself that matters; the destination is immaterial, unreachable. The real point of the journey is the change, the transformation that it engenders in the journeyer.

It follows that a religion that finds expression only in *stabilitas* may prove stagnant or even stillborn. It is the endless stirring of the waters – however apparently foolish or pointless – that keeps us climbing, searching, desiring.

The fate of the genius in the system of human knowledge is amazing and instructive. These sufferers chosen by God, doomed to destroy in the name of movement and reconstruction, find themselves in a paradoxical state of unstable equilibrium between a longing for happiness and the conviction that happiness, as a feasible reality or state, does not exist. (Tarkovsky, 1986:53)

Here, in a nutshell, is the predicament of the Stalker, and the plot of the film named for him. The happiness for which the genius longs while always suspecting it may not exist is clearly the fulfilment of deepest desires available apparently in the Room at the heart of the Zone. It is also the goal of Gregory's Moses who is never able to cease in his progress towards the unattainable, the unfulfillable desire.

I suggest this has a bearing on how we use and hear 'journey' language in a contemporary faith context. As Joanna Collicutt (2015) has recognised, for many, this language will be used to describe a simple journey to faith:

The life of faith involves goal-*directed* behavior; it has a route and destination. So one way of understanding growth [in Christian life and faith] is as progress along the route and towards the destination. (Collicutt, 2015:77; Collicutt's italics)

Later, Collicutt elaborates on the notion of journey, and appears to reconsider what 'direction' in this context might actually look like. She focuses on the descriptions of journeys in the gospels.

These journeys [in the gospel narratives] are very rarely in a straight line; they are full of diversions, there is often some backtracking and, as in the journey to Emmaus, the destination sometimes changes. A key feature of many of these journeys is turning or returning. (Collicutt, 2015:79)

Likewise, as the Stalker tells his companions, 'in the Zone old traps vanish, new ones take their place; the old safe places become impassable, and the route can be either plain and easy, or impossibly confusing.' (Tarkovsky, 1999:395)

What Tarkovsky appears to be suggesting, what Gregory of Nyssa is describing in his *Life of Moses*, perhaps what the writers of the gospels imply by the use of journeying in the Jesus narratives, is that faith is itself a journey of endless transformation; it is an adventure. What does this mean in terms of the current language of discipleship? For a start, it suggests we should risk abandoning the teleological approach; it is not the destination gives this journey meaning; there is no Room waiting for us at the heart of the Zone, no definitive answer. This is not as bleak as it sounds; in fact, as I shall try to show, I believe it is a blessing.

Three

Whether or not the Zone really is the site of something alien or miraculous, the Stalker's faith in it is the subject of the film. It is the glue that holds this desperate man together. He has gambled his marriage and staked his life, his freedom on the impossible, the unprovable, the absurd. He is the dramatic realisation of what Kierkegaard famously calls the Knight of Faith:

On this the knight of faith is clear: all that can save him is the absurd; and this he grasps by faith. (Kierkegaard, 1985:75-76)

Faith for the Stalker is not a source of power or strength. Faith does not make the journey possible; this is a journey through the impossible. Faith does not make the journey easier; trial is of this journey's essence. Faith does not reveal the journey's goal; ultimately the goal is unattainable. Faith is folly, literally the act of a fool.

It is only by being foolish, and faithful that we can begin to refresh Gregory of Nyssa's notion of faith as endless ('endless' as in never-ending but also as in goal-less) journey through a creation / a zone characterised by confusion, absence, and doubt. (As the disasters that beset the filming of *Stalker* ultimately proved a spur, a source of hope, so perhaps these seemingly negative notions of folly, risk, absence and doubt might help Christianity speak more hopefully and meaningfully to postmodern generations suspicious of claims to authoritative, objective truth, to definitive answers, to catechisms and formularies.)

Following his fruitless trip into the Zone, defeated and in despair, the Stalker is tenderly put to bed by his Wife. Like a tearful child, he rails against the Writer and the Professor for their faithlessness:

Calling themselves intellectuals, those writers and scientists. They don't believe in anything! They've got the organ with which one believes atrophied for lack of use. They know they were 'born for a purpose', 'called upon'! Can people like that believe in anything? (Stalker, 1979)

The 'most awful' thing for the Stalker is people's lack of need, their very strength in purpose and calling. They have mistaken needlessness for strength when they should have recognised precisely the opposite: that real strength lies in need – for faith.

The character of the Stalker is in every single scene of the film, except now in the final few minutes, he disappears, heartbroken, from the story. The story thus far has been almost exclusively male; but in the final two scenes we are alone first with the Stalker's wife, and then with their daughter. The wife speaks directly to us, into the camera. She confesses tearfully:

You had already learned, I expect, that he's God's fool. The whole neighbourhood was laughing at him. He was such a pitiful bungler.... But he just came up to me and said, "Come with me." And off I went. And I've not regretted it once. Not once. (Tarkovsky, 1999:415)

Reconceiving faith as folly, as destinationless journey, rather than being an admission of failure is in fact a confirmation if its fundamental nature – 'as the substance of things hoped for, the evidence of things that appear not.' (Heb. 11:1)

The substance of things hoped for, evidence of that which appears not: this could be a description of the Zone, a definition of film, an affirmation of faith. All three.

Colin Heber-Percy

Bio:

Colin is a professional screenwriter, a priest in the Church of England, and an academic. His screenwriting work (mainly for television, and mainly historical drama) has won many awards and been shown all over the world. In 2012 he wrote the BBC's Easter drama, *The Preston Passion*, and he continues to lecture and publish on spirituality, mission, and the relationship between faith and culture.

Abbreviations:

AS *Acta Sanctorum*. Edited by J. Bolland & G. Henschen. 71 vols. Antwerp, 1685
PG *Patrologia graeca*. Edited by J.-P. Migne. 162 vols. Paris, 1857-1886
PL *Patrologia latina*. Edited by J.-P. Migne. 217 vols. Paris, 1844-1864

Bibliography:

Collicutt, J. (2015) *The Psychology of Christian Character Formation*. London. SCM Press.

Gregory of Nyssa (1978) *The Life of Moses*. Translated by Abraham Malherbe & Everett Ferguson. New York. Paulist Press.

Gregory of Nyssa (1979) *From Glory to Glory: Texts from Gregory of Nyssa's Mystical Writings*. New York. St. Vladimir's Seminary Press.

Kierkegaard, S. (1985) *Fear and Trembling*. Translated by Alastair Hannay. Penguin.

Tarkovsky, A. (1986) *Sculpting in Time: Reflections on the Cinema*. Translated by Kitty Hunter-Blair. Austin, Texas. University of Texas Press.

Tarkovsky, A. (1994) *Time within Time: The Diaries 1970-1986*. Translated by Kitty Hunter- Blair. London. Faber.

Tarkovsky, A. (1999) *Andrei Tarkovsky: Collected Screenplays*. Translated by William Powell and Natasha Synessios. Faber.

Endnotes:

1 Unless otherwise specified, all quotes from *Stalker* are from the released version available on DVD from Artificial Eye. Tarkovsky's collected screenplays (Tarkvosky, 1999) contains an earlier draft of the final screenplay.

2 Lugidus's dictum is a concise expression of Benedictine regulation. According to the Rule, everything necessary ought to be available within the walls of the monastery so that there is no need for the monks to go wandering about outside (vagandi foras), which is completely unprofitable for their souls (omnino non expedit animabus eorum). (Benedict, PL66:900D)

Colin Heber-Percy

Map

We're lost. Admit it. Fingers stained
with blackberry juice trace routes across the map's unfolded M.
That's the creek to our right, and look —
the best bushes with the ripest berries are all marked
helpfully. And see how the contours squeeze to show
the land rising steeply round us.
Beech and hazel and chestnut have their own symbols.
The conkers are counted out of their cases,
and marked by little flags.
It charts the position of each fallen leaf,
each limb of each beech, every dark puddle, the twists of spume in
the stream's gutters, every tussock at the water's edge. Referring
to the legend, you can pinpoint on the map
clusters of waxcaps and blewits and deceivers;
that's the sign for owl pellet,
and this for a jay's feather.
And see, even our footprints in the soft earth
are clearly marked, as a pair of dotted lines;
the very hairs on our heads are numbered.
Yet even with a map like this,
we're lost.

Faith does not make the journey possible; this is a journey through the impossible. Faith does not make the journey easier; trial is of this journey's essence. Faith does not reveal the journey's goal; ultimately the goal is unattainable. Faith is folly, literally the act of a fool.

Colin Heber-Percy

parabolic relationships: how change happens in mission

anna ruddick

Missional riddles

>>Mission often generates more questions than answers. The reality of new relationships built, groups started, life changes made in the cause of mission, confronts previous assumptions and brings new insights. The world is not always the way we thought it would be, people are infinitely surprising and the three point mission strategy we began with seems oddly irrelevant once real people are involved.

A growing awareness of the questions raised among my colleagues and friends within the Eden Network led me to start what would become a journey of discovery, researching what was actually happening in the relationships built between Eden team members and the urban community members they came to live alongside. During my research I was employed by the Eden Network in a national developmental role and was also living in an Eden area. I drew on my own professional and personal practice as a participant observer, and qualitative 'life-story' interviews with Eden team members and community members who had met Eden teams in their neighbourhoods.

Driven by the desire to understand how people change, and particularly how mission enables people to change, my work has led to some surprising insights. In this chapter I want to share some of these insights, in response to a series of missional riddles:

When is mission pastoral care?
When is a relationship a parable?
When is a recipient of mission a missioner?

A riddle is a particularly enigmatic form of speech, requiring the use of ingenuity (rather than 'knowledge' per se) in order to fathom its meaning. This need for experience, creative thinking and practical resourcefulness seems especially pertinent to mission, in which theory must engage with reality, and God is encountered along the way. In an interplay between the existing incarnational model of the Eden Network, the experience of life in urban communities, and the activity of the Spirit, a new mode of missional living is emerging. I call it missional pastoral care. This involves mutual relationships which subvert previously held understandings of the world and introduce new ways of seeing. It is these relationships which produce life change, both flourishing and ambiguity, in mission. So to begin; the first missional riddle:

When is mission pastoral care?

Clare is in her thirties and lives on an estate in Greater Manchester. She described to me the effect of meeting Eden team members in her community and going along to church with them for the first time:

I think it was the people who went there as well, it wasn't like the people you'd normally meet, they thought a lot of theirselves they thought a lot of their health you know of each other, things like that... ...there's some, ...live here there's a lot of drugs there's a lot of all sorts and you can find yourself being in there ...and you have to get yourself away from it d'y'know what I mean? But I think going to church helped me do that to think this is not all of you don't have to be like this to be cool, to be good. ...because they live here, they live in the same place you live so you can all relate I suppose. 'Cos if they say something to you, you can't [say] "oh well I can't do that 'cos I live on [this estate]" [because they] live on [the estate] as well...

Clare's story indicates the surprise, challenge, even oddness presented by Eden team members, and the way in which that prompted her to question her own beliefs about what it meant to be a 'cool' or 'good' person. Seeing this pattern repeatedly in the stories of my participants I noticed its similarity to processes in the work of Charles Gerkin, who has dominated understandings of pastoral care since the 1980s (Couture & Hunter, 1995).

Gerkin integrated insights from psychology with a Christian theological worldview and developed what he called narrative hermeneutical pastoral care. Gerkin's model is predicated on the centrality of narrative, or story, for human identity: that 'humans structure meaning and hold in coherence the diverse elements of experience by means of a narrative structure.' (1986, p. 19). Therefore he concludes that each person has a narrative 'meaning-system' which shapes our understanding of reality and how the world works and which we use to interpret our experiences. Hermeneutics is the art of interpretation. Gerkin suggests that just as we might seek to interpret the Bible, to understand its meaning for our lives today, so every person is a 'living human document' (1984, pp. 27-30). This means that understanding a person's meaning-system requires great care and attention, to enter into their worldview.

An individual's meaning-system develops throughout their life and is learned from family, friends and authorities such as church or school as well as the individual themselves as they interpret their life experiences. For example, Clare's perception of what kind of life was possible on her estate and what it meant to be 'good' was shaped by what she observed in the lifestyles of others around her. Her understanding of her own experiences and her choices were impacted by this overarching meaning-system.

Gerkin understands pastoral care as a dynamic process in which meaning-systems are challenged and changed. He suggests that personal problems stem from an inability to find coherence between experience and an individual's overarching narrative of meaning. Gerkin's model of narrative hermeneutical pastoral care seeks to provide 'dialogical space' between the Christian narrative and the life stories of individuals seeking help. The pastoral carer (in Gerkin's model, the pastor or counsellor) facilitates the dialogue, faithfully representing the Christian tradition and empathetically engaging with the narrative of the care-seeker (1997, pp. 111-113).

In order to achieve this dialogue the pastoral carer needs to achieve a 'fusion of horizons of meaning and understanding' with the care-seeker (Gerkin, 1984, p. 44); a shared language world in which both understand the other's meaning-systems. When there is mutual understanding and shared language there is potential for the care-seeker to experiment with new ways of interpreting their experiences and new ways of seeing the world. For Gerkin this is a creative, playful process and a space in which the Spirit can work (1984, p. 124) and he understands the Christian narrative as a vital source of alternative meaning, offering a 'unitary vision that is finally meaningful' (1984, p. 53). Gerkin applies his model of a fusion of horizons and 'hermeneutical play' (1984, p. 153) to professional, church-based pastoral care. However, it is also evident in the missional relationships between Eden team members and community members in which it serves the same end of meaning-making.

So, when is mission pastoral care?

When it involves the meeting of two meaning-systems in hermeneutical play.

Informed by an evangelical missional narrative, the Eden Network conceives of its work as 'urban mission' (Wilson, 2012, p. 22). This is primarily understood as sharing 'the Christian message in words and actions' (The Message Trust, 2015). But when I listened to their stories I found activity and impact which goes beyond this understanding and expectation for 'mission'. The ministry of Eden teams involves faith-sharing but it is not focused primarily on verbal evangelism. Further, it includes social action in supporting vulnerable people but that action is not instrumentalised as a means to the end of evangelism. Finally, while it often includes conversion this is not the sole aim. In order to account for the full breadth and richness of the activity of Eden teams I describe this emerging ministry practice as a new model of mission, calling it missional pastoral care.

Missional pastoral care is activity which enacts the mission of God in three specific ways:

in a holistic sharing of life for the good of one another;
in an articulation of life narratives, including faith narratives;
and in hermeneutical play, reshaping the meaning-systems of all involved.

This model encompasses the holistic understanding of mission in the practices of Eden teams alongside an emphasis on meaning-making through relationships. Which points towards the second missional riddle:

When is a relationship a parable?

John Dominic Crossan describes 'Parable' as a form of language which plays the role of subverting accepted meanings in constructed worlds (Crossan, 1988, p. 42; Gerkin, 1984, p. 161). He notes that Jesus was known among the early church as the 'Parable of God' (Crossan, 1992, p. viii). Gerkin develops Crossan's ideas and describes the pastoral counsellor as a 'parabolic figure' in that their role is to enable the process of hermeneutical play: 'changing the mythic world from inside by means of subverting it, giving it a new twist so that a fresh possibility is opened' (Gerkin, 1984, pp. 162-169).

So, when is a relationship a parable?

When it subverts in daily talk and practice the meaning-systems of participants, allowing for new meaning-systems to be constructed in words and actions.

Community member Suzy is nineteen and from Manchester; she first met the Eden team in her community when she was nine years old. Her story illustrates this 'parabolic' model of mission:

I think more having the support of people saying "look you can do it, if you put your mind to it" 'cos at home my dad was, well a lot of the time he was in the pub so I didn't have the support at home, so I end up getting it from the Eden team...

...I used to spend quite a lot of time with Lynn, I think I used to spend 4 or 5 days with Lynn after work that's just going round, going on the computer and just chilling out, having something to eat. ...Lynn was like my mum figure 'cos I never had my mum. ...me and Lynn used to go out for days out, to the shops or just chilling out in the garden. ...It was mainly chilling and talking about how my life's changing and how I was feeling at the time and how the bullying was affecting me and... my school work... Lynn helped me a lot with my school work to keep me on track outside of school, so amazing.

...Lynn and Julie eventually started involving my dad in things, so getting me and my dad to do things as parent and daughter which we hadn't done in a long time. Lynn helping my dad out with how to keep the housework on top and stuff like that, inviting him over for food... so I had the support and then I had my dad's support it's like "I want to know God now".

Suzy described frequent, varied and meaningful encounters with Eden team members. She sees Lynn and Julie as family, even parental figures and spends regular time with them relaxing, having fun, and in more purposeful activity such as school work. They evidently provided a listening role, hearing her experiences of bullying and also practically provided food, and support with household tasks for both Suzy and her dad. In Suzy's story and those of my other participants, seven elements of missional pastoral care emerged, which shaped the relationships between Eden team members and community members: difference, locality, availability, practicality, long term commitment, consistency and love. These were brought about by Eden team members' relocation to urban neighbourhoods and they enable the subversion and re-evaluation of meaning-systems which I describe as hermeneutical play.

The differences between Eden teams and community members challenge perspectives, creating awareness of alternative ways of being. As Clare described above: "I think going to church helped me do that to think this is not all of you don't have to be like this to be cool, to be good." This difference is experienced at close hand through Locality. Eden team members focus on a relatively small and defined geographical area, prioritising time in the local community and using local facilities. Alongside locality is Availability: an intentionally open orientation, rather than a lack of boundaries, which changes over time according to circumstances but maintains a commitment to hospitality and a willingness to engage. This model is fundamentally Practical, involving the action of both Eden team members and community members in programmed activity or informal friendships. Missional pastoral care subverts a person's beliefs about themselves by enacting a different story, as Eden team member Louise described:

I remember one woman who comes from quite a large family ...when I met with her, she'd talk a lot and I would listen a lot and I'd be aware that she wasn't good at listening ...but sometimes I'll be there and there'll be all together ...they'd all be like talking at one another which made me think when I meet up with her in the week even if she has just twenty minutes or an hour of someone just giving her attention and listening to what she has to say and caring ...that could be quite a big thing... (Louise, Greater Manchester)

This involves Long term commitment & Consistency, building trust and allowing for the length of time it takes for people and relationships to grow.
Finally Love in the context of missional pastoral care is an affirmation of the sense of self of each individual. Participants talked about feeling accepted, more

themselves, even as they described changing they talked about staying the same. Sixteen year old community member Jess from Yorkshire describes:

...you just feel better about yourself and half the time you're like 'I can do that', like they inspire you to do stuff...

It's like your family, like you can talk to them about anything and they wouldn't judge you, they wouldn't think owt bad, they'd just help yer and it's really good it's just like your family, that's what you need.

This affirmation of the sense of self of each individual, allows them to stay the same as they change, enabling them to re-evaluate and change elements of their meaning-system without losing its overarching coherence. Retaining a cohesive life-story in which past beliefs are accepted even if they are now set aside prevents individuals from experiencing subjective fragmentation, the distressing fracture of self-understanding. Life change is deeply rooted rather than superficial 'fitting in' with a new, aspirational community. (2014, p. 39; Gerkin, 1984, p. 69)

In missional pastoral care this kind of loving affirmation comes alongside the challenge of difference in the course of daily, informal relationships, chatting together and doing life together. The relationships themselves are parabolic with both community members and Eden team members experiencing a degree of subversion of life narratives through difference alongside a loving affirmation of the self. This results in the revising of meaning-systems to acknowledge and account for the other's experience and the shared experience built through the relationship.

The ways in which meaning-systems are reshaped, and the new ways of living which arise from this are the outcomes of missional pastoral care. This parabolic relating produces a complex good which includes a kind of flourishing alongside loss, ambiguity and limitation.

There are five interconnecting effects of missional pastoral care which constitute a kind of flourishing resonant with Grace Jantzen's definition as 'growth and fruition from an inner creative and healthy dynamic' (1998, p. 161). They are: a stronger love of self, a more positive approach to life choices, an increased ability to act, increasing awareness of a good God, and mutuality. The story of Paul, a community member from Manchester, illustrates these in his own words:

I'm not a Christian now but I spend a lot of me time with the Christians ...I do a lot of voluntary work ...I do get a lot of responsibility off 'em and obviously I appreciate that 'cos its trust and I am a trustworthy guy ...it does make you feel good because someone's trusting you with all their property...

..say if I carried on on the streets ...half of us probably be in jail now ...but knowing these and starting getting into all more activities and helping out ...I see my change, ...obviously we still went back to do our own stuff while we was with them but instead of just climb one ladder causing trouble I was climbing two. So I was still messing about causing trouble but also climbing the ladder to gain respect you know ...cos I was being with them and then ...things move on like so I was climbing two instead of one and obviously you only want to climb one ladder and I just jumped back on to the good ladder to go the good way.

God in a way does help you [find] your way through everything if you think about it but I wanna see something before I believe in him ...God's probably that one rung ahead of me, you know until actually something happens and I meet up with him, and until that day I'm always going to be one behind him...

I could stay away from [the church] for a long time... but obviously if I still got to see the people because they're good friends now, ...obviously your friends come and go but these people I've had for eight, nine, ten, some of them ...twelve years so you build a good friendship with 'em cos you know they're always going to be around, so you can trust 'em...

Paul describes the way that his life has been profoundly shaped by his experience of missional pastoral care; impacting his self-esteem, life choices and awareness of God. Across the stories of my participants these five effects were consistently present, constituting both a part of the process of missional pastoral care practice, hermeneutical play, as well as the result of it.

The other aspect of the complex good produced by missional pastoral care is loss and ambiguity. This is found in vulnerability: that of living in an urban community; of sharing your life with another person; of the long term, process nature of this model often leading to a sense that 'not enough is happening'; and of the limits of life change (Gerkin, 1984, p. 65). These ambiguities are common in experiences of mission, and are often interpreted by practitioners as failure. My research shows that rather than these effects being wholly negative, they are a necessary part of this complex good. They constitute the challenge to and breaking apart of aspects of meaning-systems without which the flourishing described above would not be possible.

Conceiving mission as meaning-making in long term relationships marked by both difference and the affirmation of self, challenges evangelical models of missional practice. In their practice, Eden teams reach beyond the Eden Network understanding of 'urban mission' which, as does much contemporary missiology, looks for conversion and progressive lifestyle change as the results of missional effort. The use of a discourse of transformation in mission enables hopes and outcomes to be discussed positively, while concealing a lack of clarity about what exactly is happening. In its emphasis on mutual meaning making and in the resulting complex good, the parabolic relationships of missional pastoral care offer an alternative understanding of mission and its outcomes. In fact they suggest a new relationship between Christians and the recipients of their mission, bringing us to the third and final missional riddle:

When is a recipient of mission a missioner?

We all bring our history, culture and background to our mission, and we all carry what James Bielo describes as 'the imagining of a missionalised subject' (2011, p. 132), or: what we imagine that the 'recipients' of our mission think, say and do. The majority of Eden team members are from broadly middle-class backgrounds, or have been enculturated into middle-class Christian norms through their conversion. Therefore they brought features of middle-class culture along with their evangelical spirituality and this lead to a degree of objectification of those in their communities. Team member Sally in her thirties and from Greater Manchester acknowledged the tensions in her early experiences of living in an urban community:

We were terrified and also not too happy with the idea of living on a council estate... when we first came here I was like "why have all these people got all these problems, why don't they just, you know, pick themselves up and get on with it".

But in building relationships with the people around them, teams discovered that they interpreted reality in profoundly different ways. Eden team members began to realise the extent to which the urban environments and experiences of deprivation of those they met had shaped them, and, significantly, the shaping stories and places in their own lives. Sally went on to reflect on the life she and her husband might have lived had they not joined an Eden team:

...I think we probably would have been just living in a little middle-class housing estate somewhere, we wouldn't have known our neighbours, probably would have friends and or family living miles away, and actually not really have a sense of community...

This reflective process involved a re-evaluation of their previously held assumptions, including a shift from perceiving the community as dangerous to feeling safe, and from seeing it as an entirely fragmented place to recognising the community spirit among many locally.

Eden team members described these changes as brought about by God, through their experience of living in an urban community. Sally has now been in her community in Greater Manchester for ten years, she says:

I think I would say that I'm a lot more understanding of the situations that people find themselves in... God's just really enabled me to see that there's so many complexities to life that mean that people find themselves in these situations and actually you just need to get alongside them and just understand that and then find a way to help them to help themselves rather than just being impatient... So I think God's really softened me around the edges with that.

Both personally and in ministry, Eden team members have allowed their experiences, understood as the activity of God, to generate insight, including theological insight. Through their encounters with urban people Eden teams have had their own meaning-systems called into question, and they attribute this to the work of God.

So, when is a recipient of mission a missioner?

When the missioner realises that their own meaning-system is also being changed in the course of their

Anna Ruddick

missional relationships, and that this is the work of God, in them, through those they have met.

Missional pastoral care results in the creation of a community of mutuality, in which all participate in hermeneutical play. Eden team member Sally reflected on the way that she and her husband have been changed through their experience:

...the sense of community is fantastic... we've always had nice neighbours... so I think that's probably changed us 'cos I think we would have just come home every night and shut the door and not really thought about anybody else... we always kind of reckoned that... we would have ended up being just a little cocoon together if we hadn't been involved in these things... it sort of forces you to bring people into your home doesn't it and to really put yourself in their shoes...

Another Eden team member, Adam, recounts the effect of mutuality on him in the context of community activism as he discovered his local residents' association:

...they're one of the best groups of people I've met because they're so desperate to see change... it just makes me excited that we're not doing this alone, we're doing this in partnership with people that live in the area already that are already making a change. So I think, you know, when I first started Eden it was like "we are the people with the answers to the change" but actually people in the community hold the answers...

These stories show that both Eden team members and community members experience personal change as a result of hermeneutical play.

In this research it was important to me to hear from community members about their experiences of the Eden Network's mission. As I have developed missional pastoral care as a description of missional activity, community member's stories have defined the mission they have 'received', and its outcomes, alongside those of Eden team members. This is an intentional departure from top-down models of mission in which practitioners are trained to implement a defined model and the recipients are largely invisible in the process.

What has become evident in the experiences of Eden teams is that 'recipients' of mission are not invisible or passive. Whilst some models of mission may tend towards objectification (Rooms, 2015, p. 107), this is challenged by the experience of long-term, incarnational, mission practitioners who have to contend with the responses of so-called recipients whether they want to or not. Allowing these experiences, along with the perspectives of 'recipients', to inform understandings and models of mission can ensure that the church does not miss the work that God would do in us, through those we seek to 'reach'.

In order to engage in meaning-making a relationship must be developed which is mutual, which involves difference and which is defined by a loving affirmation of the 'other'. This suggests that models of mission which seek transformation but fail to enable this kind of relationship will not significantly impact the meaning-system of the missionised other. They risk having little impact at all, or simply leading to 'fitting in', rather than authentic and lasting life change. In this conception of mission both practitioners and recipients are on the receiving end of God's missional activity in the world and are changed in the process of their relationships. This makes the categories of missioner and recipient redundant in the building of mutual communities of care which are a foretaste of the kingdom of God.

Having posed three missional riddles and answered them with the experiences of Eden team members and urban community members the inventiveness required in pioneering missional practice is, I hope, self-evident. By letting ourselves be led by a mysterious God-on-mission, and by retaining a curiosity about what might be, we can participate in mission as both practitioner and recipient. Seeking the renewal of our own meaning-systems through mutual relationships with people who are different to ourselves. Missional pastoral care as an emergent model of mission among members of the Eden Network and urban community members has the potential to address the unhelpful dichotomies between mission and discipleship, kingdom and church and evangelism and social action, wrapping them up together in God's expansive work in the world.

Bio:

Dr Anna Ruddick is a freelance community theologian and researcher working to resource the church in its engagement with communities. Anna currently represents Livability, as Community Engagement Associate, and Urban Life as a Core team member. She is also a Research Fellow at Bristol Baptist College, and a trustee of the William Temple Foundation. Living in Leicester and working nationally, Anna is an active reflector who facilitates theological reflection and learning by coaching leaders. She leads learning processes for congregations, and enables strategic development in Christian organisations that are seeking to deepen and strengthen their relationships with their local community.

Bibliography:

Bielo, J. (2011). *Emerging Evangelicals: Faith, Modernity and the Desire for Authenticity.* New York: University Press.

Couture, P. D., & Hunter, R. J. (1995). *Pastoral Care and Social Conflict.* Nashville: Abingdon Press.

Crossan, J. D. (1988). *The Dark Interval: Towards a Theology of Story (Vol. 56).* Sonoma: Eagle Books.

Crossan, J. D. (1992). *In Parables: the Challenge of the Historical Jesus.* Sonoma: Eagle Books.

Gerkin, C. V. (1984). *The Living Human Document.* Nashville: Abingdon Press.

Gerkin, C. V. (1986). *Widening the Horizons Pastoral Responses to a Fragmented Society.* Philadelphia: Westminster Press.

Gerkin, C. V. (1997). *An Introduction to Pastoral Care.* Nashville: Abingdon Press.

Jantzen, G. M. (1998). *Becoming Divine: Towards a Feminist Philosophy of Religion.* Manchester: University Press.

Rooms, N. (2015). Missional Gift-Giving: A Practical Theology Investigation into what Happens when Churches Give Away "Free" Gifts for the Sake of Mission. *Practical Theology* Vol.8 No.2, 99-111.

Sremac, S. (2014). Faith, Hope, and Love: A Narrative Theological Analysis of Recovering Drug Addicts' Conversion Testimonies. *Practical Theology* 7.1, 34-49.

SteinhoffSmith, R. (1995). The Politics of Pastoral Care: An Alternative Politics of Care. In P. D. Couture, & R. J. Hunter, *Pastoral Care and Social Conflict* (pp. 141-151). Nashville: Abingdon Press.

The Message Trust. (2015, June 4). Home: The Message Trust. Retrieved from The Message Trust: http://www.message.org.uk/

Wilson, M. (2012). *Concrete Faith.* Manchester: Message Publications.

liberate or

stiny

I hope, I hope

WE'RE ALL DOO
YET HOPE HAS RISEN

All I can ever do is put one foot in front of the other
So far I have always taken me where I need t

's child -
Beyonce's a bit of
al right!

I don't travel alone
travel with

NS20

The future he

People are important
but places!

사랑과
평화

愛と平和.

NO-WHERE
NOW-HERE
AND NOW EVER IS
... NO WHERE BUT
HERE

2+2 = 6 oR

We are all immortal
if only for a life.

I MAKE
ur OWN

... It's

in
MY
HANDS. ®

He
gusts
mi bougrofo
Enjoy the journey,
as the summit might not
be what or how you imagine

NO IT ISN'T
TRUST ME

I agree th

I agree and more...

ll come back to Europe again!
ll find a new love! Alice
You'll die lonely?

Aloha!
Love the
V&A

My Nasseb

Rather
Use
Than
Fame

A great poe
one said
'Her mother said
'Don't eat with
your fingers' OR
said ridiculous
Rose-so
she ate with
her toes.

ARCHITECTURE
IS LIFE

AND A LIFE
WORTH LIVING

you said it would be
MOST of THE TIME

www.tendencias.tv

making
history

ich liebe
du

Claire would
say
Live in the
moment.
I agree.

do less.

Lovely
to c.u. again!

VIRAL WA

LIVE BEYOND
THE MOMENT

Tomorrow starts TODAY!!

stop thinking
start playing

become
famous!

Affirmation of the sense of self of each individual allows them to stay the same as they change, enabling them to re-evaluate and change elements of their meaning-system without losing its overarching coherence.

Anna Ruddick

future present: physical graffiti workshop

rachel griffiths

>>My contribution to the
Future:Present conversation took the
form of a theatre workshop. As a group
we thought about issues and situations
we wanted to change, by means of
making still images - sometimes known
as 'tableaux'. We looked, imagined the
change, altered our positions, and
were able to see the future played out
in front of us.

This way of working comes from the work and practice of Augusto Boal. Boal
was a Brazilian theatre director and maker, exiled from Brazil in the 1950's for
his political views. He worked primarily among poor, marginalised communities,
often in the countryside where the status of those people and the rights over
their land were fragile. Boal invented the Theatre of the Oppressed, inspired by
the work of his great friend Paolo Freire, and his seminal book *The Pedagogy of
the Oppressed*. Boal believed:

*...the humanisation of the dispossessed...begins with the restoration of the
artistic capacity within each person. (Boal,1998:40)*

Boal's form of theatre established participants as authors of their own work,
while spectators (whom he referred to as spect-actors) became actively
engaged in the process of watching and participating, to the point where they
were permitted not only to comment on the action, but to stop it part way
through and suggest alternative narratives.

It is this alternative narrative that we wanted to explore in our workshop. What
preoccupies us? What do we dream of for our world, locally, nationally, globally?
Where do we want to see change? How can we be agents of that change?

We were far from oppression in rural Brazil but I have seen Boal's practice work
in various contexts – a slum in India; a business room in Switzerland ; London
schools. So we gave it a try in Oxford.

The Mechanics of the Session

We were a group of around 12 people. And we began – after a quick introduction – by making some still images of familiar situations: a surprise birthday party; a family photograph; a bus stop.

The way to build these images is for one person to begin by taking up a position in the space. Everybody else watches and then begins, one at a time to respond to what they see, by adding themselves into the image. Eventually it builds into something we all recognise. It is simple, and requires nothing but a willingness to take part.

I like the family photograph example because it can be run a few times and each time the family is very different. People place themselves in that image in a variety of ways. They bring their own truth to the image, or they are free to play with being someone very different in the story of the image they create. Whatever happens, there is always a family image we recognise, whether or not it's one we want to belong to!

From this I asked someone in the group to share an issue they had brought with them to this day of imagining God's dream for the future and how we might be involved in bringing that into being. An offer came: what can we do about sex-trafficking of young women?

So first, we stated the facts, in an image: I asked the person who had offered the idea to 'mould' – as though she were a sculptor – another participant into the shape of this issue as it sits in her mind. (The person being sculpted needs to give permission to be touched and in so doing, agrees to respond to the guidance of the sculptor.) She did this – and we observed a person on their knees, head down, oppressed.

Our quest then was to imagine this image resolved; to see the hope we reach for in imagining another way. Again, the person who offered the situation was invited to take other participants and place them in the space to build the image. She added three more people in a line – each one's physicality demonstrating a step towards a final image of freedom – standing up, looking upwards, arms stretched out.

I asked our author how she felt looking at this. This is a crucial question to ask someone who has boldly shared hope in something they have not yet seen. Looking at the image she had created with four willing participants, she told us she felt emotional to witness the change she longs for, being reflected back to her. The next stage in this work would be to ask ourselves what it takes to move from that oppressed state to one of freedom. Again, we do not pull ourselves away from the physical and start a discussion. Instead we anchor our words in what we see. For example, "we need to help the oppressed person lift her head"; "She needs to stand up. She can't do that alone so she needs someone to help her." and so on. This way, we build the narrative of what we might in fact do to effect the change we have imagined and seen in front of us.

With the effect of this powerful image in our thinking and our emotions engaged through its truth, we cleared the space and this time I suggested we build a group image. So we did not have one author/sculptor. We chose our title and began to build it as co-authors. I encouraged the group to use different levels according to their physical ability – standing, sitting, crouching, lying down. Again – no words. All done in silence.

A picture was created of people gathered at a Christening, the focal point being the baby and family. Around them people positioned themselves in a variety of ways of belonging. At this point I invited people to say a word or a few words to describe how they felt in the position they had adopted. A memorable thought emerging from this came from people who appeared visually to be on the outer edges of the group, but felt they belonged to it. Which helped us to talk through different ways of belonging and how community means different things to different people.

Our workshop was short – just one hour, allowing us just to touch on ways to explore dreams and imagination. With more time, we would press in to one image, developing it, questioning the theme. We could work as a group or with one or more people as authors. There is truth to be found in both approaches. Indeed it is useful to have an outside eye. In our group, one person chose not to place herself in the images. So I asked her what she could see. This is a great question – what do you see?

I am a strong believer in finding truth and unearthing further questions using this physical language from theatre. On a truly pragmatic note, it provides a short-cut to the heart of a discussion. We don't talk around the issue, we look at the issue and it provides us with the springboard into a deeper place of exploration. And it saves time!

More poetically perhaps, we are all invited to participate and no one is in charge. No one is more eloquent than the next person. No one's voice is louder and we are all authors. Every human being has within them artistic capacity. Finally, we do not walk away wondering what is possible. We leave having represented possibility in our body, having sensed it. It is imprinted in us in some way, and therefore we are enabled to take the next step in the journey towards bringing that possibility into being.

Bio:

Rachel Griffiths has made theatre with different communities of people: primary and secondary school children; men and women in business; women and girls in India; young women in Bolivia; refugees in the Calais Jungle camp.

She is active locally as a member of her neighbourhood forum and Chair of a community group working to resettle a Syrian refugee family into the neighbourhood.

Rachel believes in motivating local people, neighbours and friends to work together for the common good.

Bibliography:

Boal, A. 1998. *Legislative Theatre*. Abingdon, Oxon: Routledge. Translated by Adrian Jackson.

Rachel Griffiths

participatory theatre project - private issues in public spaces

with women in Chennai, India,
supported by Karunalaya.
http://www.karunalaya.org

Photos by Virginie Vlaminck.

re-imagining christ as the coming girl: an advent experiment

nicola slee

Nicola Slee

Introduction

>>I want to insist on the urgency of dreaming as an imaginative work to which Christians are called and, in this essay, to engage in an experimental act of dreaming of the coming of God in female form, entering our world as a girl. If this strikes the reader as a bizarre or even improper experiment, I crave your indulgence as I seek to make my case for this being a proper theological endeavor, grounded in Scripture and Christian tradition, and one which may make a significant contribution to Christian faith and practice today.

First I will sketch out the central role of dreams and imagination in Christian life, after which I will trace the notion of God coming in female flesh in Christian theology, not only in contemporary feminist theology, but also in more ancient times.[1] I will suggest that the eschatological dimension of Christian faith – particularly evident in the Advent season, but a core strand of biblical faith – invites us to look forward with anticipation and expectation to the coming of Christ in novel and unexpected ways.

I will suggest that, whilst the Jesus of history was male, Jewish, Palestinian and young, the Christ/a of faith can – and indeed, must – manifest in a much more expanded repertoire of human faces and forms, if different groups of people throughout the world are to know themselves 'made in the image of God' and access the truth of the incarnation in their own flesh and lives. Whilst the idea of a female Christ figure – the so-called Christa – has been developed over a number of decades in feminist theology out of its more ancient lineage, the notion of Christa as a girl, is rarely heard or developed, reflecting the lack of attention to the lives, needs and gifts of girls in feminist theology, as well as in theology more broadly.

I will argue that there are particular political and theological reasons for developing the notion of Christa[2] as a girl, not least as a contribution to a more authentic theology of childhood within the Christian community.

The urgent work of dreaming

Common parlance tends to speak of 'dreamers' as those who are not in touch with reality, drifting and dreaming their lives away, living in a fantasy world of make-believe. Yet Christian faith holds dreaming in high esteem. From Jacob to Daniel, from Joseph of Nazareth to Pilate's wife, the Bible is full of stories of dreams and dreamers; it is a primary means by which God communicates to people – and not only to people of faith. Whilst Jesus does not speak of dreaming directly, many of his parables have the quality of intense, surreal dreams.

Throughout the ages, poets and theologians, amongst others, exemplify this work of dreaming: they are those who imagine the world, God and human beings, not merely as they are but as they might be. Imagination is a profoundly prophetic faculty – the vision of what might be critiques and judges the corruption of the present and the failures of the past. Our imagination is the faculty of transcendence, that capacity within us for reaching above and beyond the limitations of the present. Whilst the body can be imprisoned, tortured and killed, the imagination cannot be owned by anyone, which is why totalitarian regimes tend to fear and seek to eliminate artists, poets and people of religious faith. They know that imagination is a dangerous faculty of freedom.

Imagination is vital for feminists and for any group who do not wish to put up with present political reality. Patriarchy, colonialism, racism and every other system of oppression will not be overcome by brute force, strategy or intellectual argument so much as by a radical reclaiming of language, symbol and story to articulate an alternative reality. Feminists are those who dream that the world might be different from its present rule by male power and its endemic violence and misogyny. They seek to tell new stories, or to articulate old stories in new ways, in order to imagine what the world might look like if women's experiences were taken seriously, if women and girls were assumed to possess agency to claim and use their own power, if women and girls were made, equally with men and boys, in the image of God – as Christians surely believe they are.

So I invite you to come with me, in this article, in an exercise of feminist imagination, a work of dreaming of how God might come to us in new forms and ways, and specifically as a girl. I offer this experiment in both playful and deadly serious mode. It is an invitation to perceive God incarnate amongst us in new ways and to glimpse anew the sacral nature of human flesh; specifically, it is an attempt to lift up the bodies and lives of girls as holy and precious, capable of imagining and reflecting the incarnate God. I intend this experiment to be subversive of tired and stock ways of thinking about the advent of God in Christ, an exercise in free thinking which may be challenging, critical and hopeful.

In many ways, the idea that God may be amongst us in female form is hardly a novel idea. Yet the specific notion that Christ/a might be born amongst us as a girl, and attention to the image of the girl as a symbol for Christ, is more unusual. As Anne Phillips and others[3] have pointed out, the faith lives of girls have been neglected in feminist as well as mainstream theology until very recently; attention to the specific needs and experiences of girls, as well as the gifts they might bring to Christian faith, has been rare. I hope this experiment in imagining Christ/a as a girl may help to reverse this trend.

'It's a girl!'

There's a cartoon which I've seen both online and in various versions as a Christmas card; it shows Mary and Joseph in the stable, with the crib centre-stage. Mary has a startled look on her face as she gazes into the crib, and the speech bubble declares, "It's a girl!" Here's my version of this, as a poem:

> The news spread like wildfire.
> Sages were perplexed.
> Astronomers recalculated their stars.
> Shepherds sloped back to their charges.
> Only the midwives smiled their knowing smiles.
> And the angels crowded round,
> singing "Glory! Glory!" [4]

The cartoon works precisely because it is amusing, if not shocking, to imagine Christ coming as a girl. But why is it such a startling idea? There's another, rather less well-known version of this joke, which tells how God did come as a girl, and no-one took the slightest bit of notice of anything she said or did, nothing got passed on or written down, so God had to start again and send a boy. And the rest is history.

Come as a girl.
I did. Nobody noticed.

Come as a girl.
I do. Open your eyes, your mind, your stoppered ears.

Come as a girl.
**I will. I am still arriving among you,
looking for a safe place to be born,
a welcome, a home.**[5]

What if?

Could God have come as a girl? Whilst to some Christians this seems a ludicrous notion, and I have met those who suggest it is blasphemous even to ask the question, the issue was taken seriously by early theologians and was a matter of considerable debate, particularly amongst medieval theologians. As Janet Martin Soskice puts it, 'The conclusion, that it was fitting that Christ be born a man, was never in doubt, yet the arguments are worth noting by anyone interested in the symbolics of sex'.[6] After reviewing a variety of these arguments, Soskice comes to the most common one, typified by Aquinas in the *Summa Theologiae*: 'Because the male excels the female sex, Christ assumed a man's nature' – though this is balanced by the additional comment, 'So that people should not think little of the female sex, it was fitting that he should take flesh from a woman'.[7] Even while the great theologian attempts to retain respect for female flesh, paralleling the body of Mary with the infant Christchild's flesh, it is clear that he still thinks, as does the little girl in her letter to God, that 'boys are best'.[8]

I want to suggest that it is not a ludicrous idea that Christ might have come – and might yet come – as a girl, but is, in fact, an idea expressive of some core Christian theological principles. In particular, the eschatological dimension of Christian faith orients us towards the endless future coming of Christ in forms and ways that will take us by surprise and for which we are not prepared. Christianity is, of course, a historical tradition with roots in a specific history – the history of Israel, as well as the history of Jesus of Nazareth and the early church; there is nothing in what I wish to propose that denies or seeks to undo that specific history. Yet the notion that Christianity is a historical tradition does not only point to its rootedness in the past; it also expresses its dynamic unfolding over time and its openness to future development. History is not only about the past, it is also about the emergent and the future forms that a tradition might take and indeed, must take, if it is not to ossify in the past.

Advent eschatology

The eschatological dimension of Christian faith comes to the fore particularly in the Advent season, when the liturgy of the church looks forward to the second coming of Christ in glory and judgement, as well as offering a period of preparation for the celebration of the first coming of Christ as a vulnerable child.

Advent is a time of preparation for the 'second' coming of Christ; and I want to say, for the third, fourth, fifth, fiftieth and hundredth coming of Christ, not in some future apocalyptic end-time, but in the real historical future that is just around the next corner, the next day or month or year. Advent is a looking forward as well as backward: it is a time to anticipate newness rather than mere repetition of the gospel story we (think we) all know and love. Above all, Advent is a dynamic period of expectation, arousal and awe for the coming of that which we do not yet know: the Christ who is not yet born amongst us, the Christ who is strange and unfamiliar to us, the Christ who comes in ever new forms, as the stranger, the incognito, the unrecognized and unwelcomed, the neglected and the marginalized.

The notion of the Christ incognito is a strong biblical theme. Jesus' teaching is full of stories about the coming one who is unexpected and unprepared for, whether this is the master who returns, unexpectedly, at midnight (Mark 13:35) or the bridegroom who appears when the bridesmaids are asleep (Matthew 25:1-13). Paul speaks of the coming of Christ as a 'thief in the night' at a time and an hour when he is least expected (1 Thessalonians 5:2). But it is not only the time that is unexpected; the form, too, of the future Christ, is strange and unexpected. This is particularly evident in the resurrection narratives in the gospels.

A recurring theme in these strange stories is the fact that the risen Christ is not recognised by his disciples (e.g. Luke 24: 13-35; John 20: 1-18; John 21: 1-8) and I want to suggest that this is a theme of core theological significance. It is more than the lack of recognition by those who are unprepared to meet one whom they believe to be dead, returned to life in their midst. There is the strong suggestion, in many of the narratives of the resurrection, that the risen Christ is strange and different from the earthly form of the historical Jesus. (S)he is the same and yet not the same. They fail to recognise him (her?) and do not know how to respond to him (her). A BBC and HBO film of Christ's passion produced in 2008, reflected this feature of the resurrection narratives by showing different actors appearing very briefly in different episodes, suggesting the fluidity of the risen Christ.[9]

This is deeply significant. The risen Christ is in continuity with the historical Jesus yet is so much more expansive. Whereas the historical Jesus was male, Jewish, Palestinian, young (yet we do not know what he looked like), the risen Christ is none of these – or all of them and more. Whereas the historical Jesus walked among us in one specific and utterly unique human body, affirming the closeness of God to all human flesh, the risen Christ cannot be confined by particularities of gender, race, age or bodily form. The forms the Christ will take are novel, strange, unrecognised, subversive, pushing the boundaries of the known and familiar. Christ may, indeed does, manifest as African, Asian, Polynesian as well as European, appearing as Black and not only white (so often we think of Jesus as white, and the image of the white Christ has reinforced white supremacy).

Christ may manifest as old (something the earthly Jesus never experienced), as disabled, blind, with mental health issues; as gay, trans or queer – and as female, as well as male. If Christ incorporates all human life and experience, and 'saves' humanity by his flesh-taking, then it must be possible to imagine Christ as female, gay, black, blind. If not, we might as well stop baptising women, Blacks, gays and disabled people (and there have been times in history as well as in the present when, of course, some of these groups have been excluded from the fellowship of the Church and denied access to God's welcome table).

Thus, at Advent most particularly, but at any time of the year, we are invited to welcome the Christ who continues to be born among us: black and white, young and old, male and female (and gender queer), in likely and unlikely places. And, as the historical Jesus was born a poor refugee amongst an oppressed and despised people, to parents whose sexual relationship was at the very least unconventional, so Christ/a continues to be born amongst us as the vulnerable, unprotected and unnoticed one dwelling amongst the poor, the despised and oppressed. It just turns out that, in our own time, this is most likely to be a girl child.

The girl child in our own time

Both at the time of Jesus and in our own world, the child remains the most powerful symbol of those who are most radically powerless and dispossessed – and the girl child very particularly. In a global setting, girls are still those most likely to be aborted or abandoned at birth, deprived of education, healthcare and basic rights, at risk of sexual and physical abuse and trafficking. There are plenty of statistics to prove it,[10] and daily on our TV screens we see and hear examples of the vulnerability and abuse of women and girls around the world. In times of war, women and girls are most likely to be raped and displaced from their homes; in so-called 'peace' time, women and girls are most at threat from domestic violence, malnourishment and slavery in their own homes.

In such a world, looking and longing for the coming of God as a girl is not simply a wishful fantasy, a joke or a feminist whim, but an urgent desire for liberation and healing for these vulnerable little ones. It is a cry to the God who identifies with the little ones and the least amongst men to come amongst us anew as a young girl, sharing the danger and the delight, the potential and the immense risk of female flesh.

As previously mentioned, the girl is a neglected site in theology – hardly visible in scripture or tradition or in contemporary theology. Anne Phillips reviews the relevant scriptural texts on girls, demonstrating how scant the material is and how, even where girls are present in scripture, they are almost always un-named and passed over as insignificant.[11] Even feminist theology has ignored girls until very recently, perhaps due to the critique of women's identities and value being limited to marriage and motherhood in patriarchy (so also, motherhood has been neglected within feminist theology).[12] Boyhood has been more visible in Christian tradition, far more imaged in paintings, stained glass and other forms of iconography through the boyhood of Christ and other significant male figures such as Moses, Samuel, David and so on.

Of course, much of the iconography of childhood in Christian tradition is deeply problematic: images of Christ as a boy are frequently sentimental and idealized, and hardly offer helpful resources for thinking about the faith lives of children, including boys, today. There is undoubtedly an urgent need to consider the faith lives of boys and to relate newly emerging masculinities to our thinking about the changing needs and gifts of boys and men within the life of the Church.[13] Yet the even greater degree of invisibility of girls within Christian faith, in a global setting of risk and danger to girlhood, points to my focus in this essay on girls specifically, rather than children more generally.

The girl as a symbol of the be-coming God

In a highly suggestive article, Marcella Althaus-Reid (one of our most daring and original theological dreamers) speaks of the girl as 'the becoming of the becoming woman, and of all becomings'.[14] The girl is poised on the threshold of womanhood, in the liminal state of pure potential, embodying the manifold choices and possibilities that lie before every human being at birth, yet may be most vulnerable to being squashed in the female child. Research conducted into the development of girls has painted a fairly consistent picture of the ways in which the freedom and experimentation of early childhood become increasingly constrained for girls as they grow closer to puberty and to taking on the expectations of adult femininity. Some research suggests that girls quite literally lose their voices as they approach puberty and become prey to adult pressures to 'tone down' their style, their bodily gestures and movements, as well as their opinions (young girls may run, climb trees, shout and swagger freely, yet this is not how 'young ladies' are expected to comport themselves).[15]

The enormous pressures on young women to look and dress in particular ways, to be small and thin and to take up little room in the world, may manifest in anorexia and other eating disorders,[16] as well as in a lack of academic and other kinds of confidence. Some girls experience a sense of dread, anxiety and depression as they approach puberty and recognize that they will be expected to conform to notions of femininity with which they do not identify. Of course, boys are also subject to very considerable social pressures to conform to dominant notions of masculinity, although these generally enshrine more agency and power than dominant notions of femininity. And of course, too, the lives of girls in many parts of the world where such research has not been conducted is even more at risk from other, more basic denial of human rights (shelter, education, food, privacy and healthcare, and so on). In so many ways, the potential of girls to become all that they have it in them to become – the full flowering of their humanity and the potential to contribute in novel and original ways to their communities and world – is threatened and undermined.

The symbol of the Christa who comes as a girl speaks into this reality at a number of different levels. First, it expresses the identification of God in Christ with the experiences of girls and, most particularly, with their struggles and suffering. God is not indifferent to such life-threatening suffering but enters into it, taking the risks and threats to life experienced routinely by girls, into God's very own flesh and being.

Second, the symbol of the Christa who comes as a girl expresses the longing of God for the survival of girls, and the commitment of God towards the salvation and flourishing of girls. Rachel Starr has recently argued for a model of salvation as survival, suggesting this is a more authentic and helpful model of salvation than many existing models rooted in violent theologies of atonement or sacrificial suffering.[17] The Christa who comes as a girl and survives all the threats to her well-being is a powerful symbol of the capacity of girls to withstand all that threatens their survival and flourishing in the world. The God who is for us stands with and alongside girls in their vulnerability and potential as they struggle against the forces of denial and death that would abort their potential before it has even begun to be released.

Third, the symbol of the Christa who comes as a girl affirms the girl as a symbol of the be-coming God. Our images and models of God function deeply at both the psychological and sociological level, as well as theologically, to model what we believe about human nature. As Mary Daly put it decades ago, 'if God is male, then the male is God' [18]; and, conversely, if God is never imaged in female terms, then women and girls do not know themselves to be made in the image of God. So the symbol of Christa as a girl speaks very powerfully of the ways in which girls may incarnate and represent God present and at work in the world.

So what?

What might it mean to take seriously the notion that young girls can represent and symbolize the coming of Christ/a in our midst? It would mean taking the gifts and experiences of girls seriously in the worship, theology and life of the church more generally; it would mean listening to them seriously and regarding them not only as 'future church' but as present church. It would mean expecting to learn and receive from girls, and not only seeing ourselves as those who teach and nurture them. It would mean committing to their full visibility in the life of the church, searching for scriptures and stories and images of girls that are positive and affirming of the potential of girls.[19] It would also mean taking seriously the risk and danger to girls in our society and world, and having courage to name these realities in Christian worship and teaching. It would mean regarding girls, as well as children generally, as theologians who might teach us as well as disciples who learn with us in the lifelong process of becoming what we are called to be.

And it would mean praying to God in female language, imagery and symbols, as we actively look for the myriad ways in which Christ/a comes to us afresh. Thus I end this essay with one such prayer which I invite readers to try praying in the season of Advent – or indeed, at any other time of the year.

> *Christa, our sister,*
> *come to us in female flesh,*
> *tasting the danger and delight of any young girl's growing;*
> *bleeding as we bleed,*
> *loving as we love,*
> *learning to claim our womanly power*
> *as God's redemptive presence in the world.*[20]

Bio:

Professor Nicola Slee is Director of Research at the Queen's Foundation for Ecumenical Theological Education and Professor of Feminist Practical Theology at the Vrije Universiteit, Amsterdam. A lay Anglican and a poet, she has published widely in the fields of feminist and practical theology, spirituality and liturgy. She is also an Honorary President of WATCH (Women and the Church).

Endnotes:

1. For a much fuller exploration of the notion of the Christa, see my *Seeking the Risen Christa* (London: SPCK, 2011).

2. In this essay, I shall use the term 'Christa' to refer to the female Christ form, whilst 'Christ/a' is an attempt to incorporate both male and female (and gender ambivalent) forms of the Christ.

3. Anne Phillips, *The Faith of Girls: Children's Spirituality and Transition to Adulthood* (Farnham: Ashgate, 2011) is a landmark text which breaks new ground in the study of the faith of girls, and I owe much to Anne for my own developing awareness of the significance of the theological study of girlhood. Most of what is in this essay is directly dependent on Anne's work. See also Dori Grinenko Baker, *Doing Girlfriend Theology: God-Talk with Young Women* (Cleveland: Pilgrim Press, 2005) and Joyce A. Mercer, *Girl Talk, God Talk: Why Faith Matters to Adolescent Girls – and Their Parents* (San Francisco: Jossey Bass, 2008).

4. 'It's a girl', in Gavin D'Costa, Eleanor Nesbitt, Mark Pryce, Ruth Shelton and Nicola Slee, *Making Nothing Happen: Five Poets Explore Faith and Spirituality* (Farnham: Ashgate, 2014): 38.

5. 'Come as a girl', in Nicola Slee, *Seeking the Risen Christa*: 33.

6. Janet Martin Soskice, *The Kindness of God: Metaphor, Gender, and Religious Language* (Oxford: Oxford University Press, 2008): 85.

7. *Summa Theologiae* 3a, 31, 4 (London: Eyre & Spottiswoode, 1964).

8. In *Children's Letters to God*, edited by Stuart Hemple and Eric Marshall (London: HarperCollins, 1976), Sylvia's letter goes 'Dear God, Are boys better than girls? I know you are one, but try to be fair'.

9. 'The Passion', by Frank Deasy, directed by Michael Offer, BBC Productions and HBO Films, originally broadcast on BBC1 in March 2008.

10. See, for example, http://www.unwomen.org/en/news/in-focus/commission-on-the-status-of-women-2012/facts-and-figures and http://www.worldbank.org/en/topic/gender/overview. Accessed 5 January 2018.

11. See Phillips, *The Faith of Girls*, 1-3, 73-4, 163-5.

12. An important exception is Bonnie J. Miller-McLamure, *Also a Mother: Work and Family as Theological Dilemma* (Nashville: Abingdon, 1994).

13. See, for example, Mark Pryce, *Finding a Voice: Men, Women and the Community of the Church* (London: SCM, 1996); David Anderson, Paul Hill & Roland Martinson, *Coming of Age: Exploring the Identity and Spirituality of Younger Men* (Minneapolis, MN: Augsberg Fortress, 2006).

14. Marcella Altaus-Reid, 'The Bi/girl Writings: From Feminist Theology to Queer Theologies', in *Post-Christian Feminisms: A Critical Approach* (Aldershot: Ashgate, 2008): 112.

15. For a comprehensive review and discussion of relevant research, see Phillips, *The Faith of Girls*, chapter 2.

16. Lisa Isherwood, *The Fat Jesus: Feminist Explorations in Boundaries and Transgressions* (London: Darton, Longman & Todd, 2008), provides a strong critique of the slimming industry aimed at young girls and endorsed by Evangelical religion, particularly in the USA.

17. Rachel Starr, *Reimagining Theologies of Marriage in Contexts of Domestic Violence: When Salvation is Survival* (London: Routledge, forthcoming).

18. Mary Daly, *Beyond God the Father: Towards a Philosophy of Women's Liberation* (London: Women's Press, 1986, 2nd edition): 19.

19. This is not easy; as already mentioned, there are very few stories about girls in the Bible and even when girls are mentioned, they are often nameless or passive objects in a male world. However, Anne Phillips highlights some possibilities, such as Hosea and Gomer's daughter Lo-ruhamah (Hosea 1: 6, 8), Namaan's (unnamed) servant girl in 2 Kings 5, the daughters of Zelophehad (Numbers 27), Jairus' daughter (Mark 5:21-43 and parallels), the servant girl Rhoda (Acts 12:13-15) and, of course, Mary the mother of Jesus, who was likely to have been little more than a teenager when she became pregnant (see Elizabeth Johnson, *Truly Our Sister: A Theology of Mary in the Communion of Saints* [New York: Continuum, 2003], part 4, for a helpful account of Mary's young life).

20. Nicola Slee, *Seeking the Risen Christa*: 148.

Whereas the historical Jesus walked among us in one specific and utterly unique human body, the risen Christ cannot be confined by particularities of gender, race, age or bodily form. The forms the Christ will take are novel, strange, unrecognised, subversive, pushing the boundaries of the known and familiar.

Nicola Slee

learning from the past to inspire the future

john drane

>>For the last fifteen years, I have been co-chair of the Mission Theology Advisory Group (MTAG) - a joint venture between the Church of England (who appoint the other co-chair, currently the bishop of Lichfield) and Churches Together in Britain and Ireland (who appointed me). We have thirteen members from a wide diversity of ecclesiastical and theological backgrounds, united by a common passion for mission.

It is often remarked that, though MTAG is embedded in institutional structures and is therefore part of 'the Establishment', it is more of a community than a committee, and it is no secret that this is one of the main reasons why I have stayed with it for so long. Theology done in community is not only a very agreeable experience but is something that models a missional way of being.

The Past: Martin Luther and his 95 theses

In autumn 2016 we discussed the possibility of doing something creative to mark the 500th anniversary of the promulgation of Martin Luther's 95 theses (or statements), which was to fall on 31st October 2017. Luther was a professor of moral theology in Wittenberg, a small German town on the banks of the river Elbe, and the story goes that he nailed his statements on the door of the Schlosskirche, otherwise known as All Saints Church. The academic world is somewhat divided on whether he actually did that, though the present day guardians of the church certainly believe he did, and it is more likely than not that the story is true as it was common practice at the time for university notices to be posted on church doors in the town. If evidence of the display of other statements is anything to go by, Luther may well have nailed his document to several doors over a period of a couple of weeks at the beginning of November in 1517.

Luther's 95 theses were of course concerned with issues relevant to his day, and though they were contentious at the time some of them would now be regarded as self-evident statements of Christian belief while others would be all but incomprehensible.[1] From our perspective the first one would hardly seem controversial with its claim that "When our Lord and Master Jesus Christ said, 'Repent', he willed the entire life of believers to be one of repentance."

But many of them were highly critical of certain practices that had become widespread in the medieval Roman church, most notably the sale of indulgences which were cash payments made to the church as an act of mercy that would allegedly enable donors or their nominees to escape punishment for their sins, or at least to reduce the length of time they might have to spend in purgatory after death. In practical terms this was a win/win situation for all concerned: the church was able to raise vast sums of money, while the faithful could accelerate their entrance into heaven. Luther challenged all this and more and the rest, as they say, is history. His 95 theses were published and distributed in many different forms throughout Europe and unleashed the cultural and religious forces that led to what we now know as the Protestant Reformation in its various manifestations.

The Present: missional questions for the 21st century

Phyllis Tickle has observed a historical pattern in which significant cultural upheavals have occurred on a cycle of some five hundred years[2] and while explanations for this phenomenon may vary, it is hard to deny the reality and one of the recurring themes in MTAG's discussions has been the way in which the turbulence of the sixteenth century is paralleled by the cultural and spiritual turmoil of our own day. STREAM is an acronym that we use to describe the various aspects of our concerns, representing the words Spirituality, Theology, Reconciliation, Evangelism, and Mission.

The first one, Spirituality, has become a major concern, as we have interacted with that significant section of the population who would describe themselves as 'spiritual but not religious' – a term that can cover everything from mindfulness and meditation to full-blown commitment to new religious movements of one sort or another, or perhaps engagement in the Sunday Assembly, whose popular media image as the 'atheist church' masks its underlying concern to celebrate whatever gives meaning and purpose to life, something that by any definition can justifiably be considered 'spiritual'.[3]

Ten years ago we produced a resource entitled 'Sense making Faith', which began as we asked ourselves what apologetics for the 21st century might realistically look like. As I recall, our initial question was to ask what we as Christians have in common with everyone else on the planet, and which could not be contradicted. The answer turned out to be our physical embodiment, and so we explored what Christian faith might look like when viewed through the lenses of our five senses (sight, touch, smell, sound, taste), to which we added imagination as a sixth sense that would animate the others.[4]

We had great fun as we explored all this in our meetings, and alongside the initial resource we ended up launching our website www.spiritualjourneys.org.uk as a vehicle for sharing many of our resources. We have continued to provide insights for understanding the spirituality of our culture, most recently with a reflection on the nature of social liturgy as displayed in the One Love Manchester concert that was staged following the bomb attack on Ariana Grande's concert in June 2017.[5]

Baggage from the past

Relating Martin Luther to these contemporary concerns was by no means without its challenges: he was a complicated individual and his personal heritage has given rise to many questions over the centuries. His own spiritual angst was very real, and his concerns with the medieval church were more than skin deep. He felt personally betrayed by his own spiritual leaders, as if they had intentionally hidden the true nature of the gospel from him in order to keep him in line.

Inevitably, when the message of God's unconditional love came to life as he read the letter to the Romans, he intuitively compared his own life-changing realization with the episode that played a correspondingly pivotal role in the life of St Paul: his encounter with the risen Christ on the Damascus Road (Acts 9:1-19). Luther had been at the end of himself, oppressed with doubt and on the cusp of suicidal despair, and it was natural for him to conclude that St Paul must have felt the same. Luther had been oppressed by the dogma of the church and disheartened by his own inability ever to live up to its requirements, so he assumed that must have been St Paul's experience as well – not in the church, of course, but in Judaism.

As a consequence, an uncritical narrative emerged in which Judaism was represented as an oppressive rule-based system making impossible demands on its followers and leading inevitably to mental and spiritual breakdown. In reality, of course, this was a caricature not only of Judaism but also of St Paul's conversion. Far from being defeated and oppressed as he travelled the road to Damascus, he was actually on a spiritual high – totally convinced that he was carrying out the will of God. The thing that brought him up short was not deliverance from institutionally-induced misery but the realization that what, on the basis of extensive study of the Hebrew scriptures, he believed to be the very epitome of obedience was actually the opposite. It was not a sense of sinful inadequacy that led to a turnaround in Paul's life, but a dramatic divine intervention – which, in a way, was also Luther's experience though for different reasons and in a different set of circumstances.

However, Luther's easy identification of Judaism with the failings of the medieval church went unchallenged, no doubt because it coincided with anti-Jewish sentiments in the wider European culture of the time. It was a short step from that to an open hostility to the Jewish people, and Luther himself was to emerge as an anti-Semitic propagandist, something that was seized upon centuries later to give a sense of legitimacy to the Nazi movement.[6] He also adopted a somewhat cavalier attitude to the Biblical canon, famously dismissing James as "an epistle of straw" because he perceived it to be in contradiction to the teachings of Paul, and ending up with a position not too dissimilar from that of the second century heretic Marcion, with a "canon within a canon" in which anything that might be perceived as promoting institutional structures was regarded as too close to the Roman church, and therefore to be downgraded if not eliminated entirely – the writings of Luke being foremost among them, along with 1-2 Timothy, Titus, Ephesians, and one or two other minor writings, as well as the Old Testament.[7] Until the late twentieth century this approach influenced much Biblical scholarship.

Reimagining: past-present-future

It was in full knowledge of this potentially problematic legacy that the members of MTAG set about identifying a good way in which to mark this significant anniversary, in which the inadequacies of the past could be acknowledged while recognizing the eschatological core of the gospel, inviting us to a new future of transformation and forgiveness rather than dwelling on the errors of the past. Given that we exist to be a theological think tank on mission, the idea of 95 missional theses for the 21st century seemed an obvious way to go. Having an idea – even a good idea – is no guarantee of success, and we soon realized that it would take a degree of ingenuity and imagination to carry this through.

It was easy enough to decide on practicalities: we would be sharing all this on social media, so Twitter's word limit (140 characters at the time) would determine how long each one of the theses could be, and we agreed to begin them with the statement "we believe in a church that...". We also wanted each one to have an accompanying Bible passage and a picture. All that was quite straightforward. It was much more challenging to come up with 95 statements each of which would genuinely say something different, and by the time we got to about thirty of them I was starting to wonder if that was going to be possible.

The turning point came when we decided to organize them according to the five marks of mission.[8] That not only provided a structure but also meant that we would be affirming and expanding on a way of looking at mission that already had wide acceptance in churches around the world. We decided to begin sharing our missional theses 95 days before the actual anniversary on 31st October, one a day and – in order to maintain interest – to do so in a random order. The first statement on 28th July 2017 was "We believe in a church that tells the world 'God is love' (1 John 4:8)". No-one had any idea what to expect, but by the time we reached the end of October there were multiple discussions taking place all over social media, many of them well beyond our initial posts as people retweeted and shared in different ways and started their own conversations.[9]

In addition to our own direct posts and those of individuals who followed us, Messy Church published their own versions specially reworked for children, while various websites related to the 500th anniversary of the Reformation also featured them. Many local churches made them available in various forms, while others used them as a basis for study groups. At least one Anglican diocese (Birmingham) adopted them for clergy study days, and several cathedrals displayed them in various forms.

From the point of view of the Mission Theology Advisory Group, this was a remarkably successful venture, not only stretching our own creativity in the process of refining the wording of these statement but also substantially increasing our own exposure to the wider church. Reactions on Facebook are especially noteworthy, with the conversation taken up in 45 countries and including significant numbers of non-Christians as well as church people.[10]

The detailed analysis of how these statements were taken up and discussed is too extensive to report in detail here, but looking at both Facebook and Twitter there is a discernible pattern which arguably reveals something of the missional context in which we find ourselves. The top thesis on Twitter was "we believe in a Church that is more concerned with the mystery that is God than with its own success (Hebrews 2. 1-11)", while the top two on Facebook were "we believe in a Church that is more concerned to ask the right questions than to impose the right answers (Proverbs 5.1-4)" and "we believe in a Church that can laugh at itself, learn from its foolishness, where fun is a key spiritual discipline (Zechariah 8.4-5)".[11]

Not surprisingly, Twitter users (where our followers are overwhelmingly clergy and other church people) appreciated being told that "we believe in a Church which loves, nourishes and cares for its leaders (Hebrews 13.17-20)" and also emphasized the importance of partnership, listening to other voices, and a sense of humility in missional attitudes. They showed least interest in engaging with those theses that mentioned sin, repentance, failings, or relationships and – surprisingly! – Jesus. Facebook respondents (a much broader international group) embraced those theses that emphasized questioning, enjoyment, exploration, crossing boundaries, creativity and love – and were least concerned about personal responsibility, social action and care for others.

Challenges and opportunities

This is being written just a month after the anniversary date, and more thought needs to be given as to what we might learn from all this. One obvious thing relates to communication styles. It can be taken for granted that social media has an important role to play in sharing the Christian message – not just within the church but to the wider world. Every thesis could have given rise to a substantial explanation, and while it was at times frustrating to try and condense things into just 140 characters, doing that was a good discipline in itself and the succinct nature of the theses made them more accessible to more people than would otherwise have been the case. There is something here about learning how to explain ourselves in simple ways that others can relate to.

Beyond that, however, the way that these theses were taken up and talked about tells us something about the wider culture. It was significant that one of the top statements focused on "the mystery that is God". Do we spend too much time talking about ourselves to ourselves when we should really be talking about God to those who are not yet people of faith? It is easy to ask the question, harder to discipline ourselves to focus on what is truly important. But there is a hunger for mystery in a culture that at times can seem exclusively materialistic – whether that hunger is expressed in terms of conspiracy theories, zombies, new spiritualities, or the search for personal healing and social transformation.

That was reinforced by the level of engagement with the need to ask the right questions rather than imposing our own answers. Is cultural change now so rapid and unpredictable that our calling is to know how to ask the right questions, to articulate them in simple ways for others, and to walk alongside people as they struggle to make sense of it all? I was also struck by the enthusiasm for "a Church that can laugh at itself, learn from its foolishness, where fun is a key spiritual discipline".

It reminded me of *The Dream of Wesley Frensdorff*, one time bishop of Nevada, in which he not only emphasized fun as a key spiritual discipline but (too radically for some) concluded "let us dream of a people called to recognise all the absurdities in ourselves and in one another, including the absurdity that is LOVE, serious about the call and the mission but not, very much, about ourselves, who, in the company of our Clown Redeemer can dance and sing and laugh and cry in worship, in ministry and even in conflict."[12] Could it be that mention of Jesus failed to engage in the way we might have hoped because of the vacuous images that many people have of him? Do we need to learn how to tell the story in ways that go well beyond the depictions in Hollywood movies or stained glass windows that are all that many people know of him?

One thing that was well appreciated was the inclusion of Biblical references – something that unintentionally highlighted the general lack of Bible knowledge even among Christians. One person was typical of many when they wrote "I had never looked at the book of Proverbs before – it's amazing". Considering that Proverbs is one of the more straightforward bits of scripture, that was a revealing statement – and it was by no means unique. We intentionally chose to include what might be regarded as less obvious Bible passages, from books such as Lamentations or Deuteronomy, but the lack of Bible knowledge obviously runs deep even among Christians. How can we connect the message of scripture with the concerns of people today?

A comment from a group of theological students identified a not unrelated question as they asked in relation to all the theses "why don't we get to discuss things like this?" – something that took me by surprise, but raises a question for theological educators about the sort of things that are being discussed and how they equip people for ministry within the church, let alone in the wider culture. I wonder if we spend too much time on questions akin to "how many angels can dance on the head of a pin?" and as a consequence find ourselves – at least in relation to mission in the wider culture – in a place not unlike the king in Hans Christian Andersen's story of the emperor's new clothes?

There were many thousands of conversations that could be referenced here, but one other recurring theme is worth mentioning. It surfaced as people asked why we were doing this, and how we ourselves understood our own theses. In a nutshell, were we describing the church empirically, as it is, or were we describing it aspirationally, as it ought to be? That came as no surprise to me: it is a tension that I live with every day. But I struggle – as I imagine many do – when someone says "I would love to belong to a Church like this, but I have had to leave because it isn't anything like this." It reminded me of a woman I was once involved with in a pastoral situation who said to me that she would love to follow Jesus "but I have enough problems already in my life without getting involved with the church". That is perhaps the biggest missional challenge of all, and takes us full circle back to Martin Luther, for his fundamental complaint was that the church had failed to be itself and had ended up denying its own core values.

Bio:

John Drane has spent much of his adult life wrestling with the challenge of being a Christian in a rapidly changing culture, and has written many books on missional topics as well as three best-selling books on the Bible which have been translated into more than ninety languages. He teaches the Bible in Context module for the CMS pioneer course and is also co-chair of the Church of England's Mission Theology Advisory Group as well as being a trustee of Fresh Expressions and chair of its *mission shaped ministry* board. He is married to Olive, and they are both Fellows of St John's College, Durham.

John Drane

Endnotes:

1. Luther's theses can be found at http://www.luther.de/en/95thesen.html

2. *The Great Emergence: how Christianity is changing and why* (Grand Rapids: Baker Academic 2008)

3. https://www.sundayassembly.com/

4. Anne Richards (ed), *Sense making Faith: body, spirit, journey* (London: CTBI 2007)

5. https://youtu.be/PD2c-2FMGqQ

6. In 1543, Luther published a substantial volume with the title *On the Jews and their Lies*. It played a prominent part in Hitler's Nuremberg rallies and was distributed to Nazi supporters. Lutheran churches around the world have more recently dissociated themselves from this aspect of his legacy.

7. "In a word, St. John's Gospel and his first epistle, St. Paul's epistles, especially Romans, Galatians, and Ephesians, and St. Peter's first epistle are the books that show you Christ and teach you all that it is necessary and salvatory for you to know, even if you were never to see or hear any other book or doctrine. St. James' epistle is really an epistle of straw, compared to the others, for it has nothing of the nature of the gospel about it." See Luther's *Works*, vol. 35, *Word and Sacrament I* (Philadelphia: Fortress Press 1960), 395–97.

8. (1) To proclaim the good news of the Kingdom; (2) To teach, baptise & nurture new believers; (3) To respond to human need by loving service; (4) To transform unjust structures of society, to challenge violence of every kind and pursue peace and reconciliation; (5) To strive to safeguard the integrity of creation, and sustain and renew the life of the earth. For more on the marks, http://www.anglicancommunion.org/identity/marks-of-mission.aspx

9. The full list of 95 missional theses (as well as other MTAG resources) can be found at https://ctbi.org.uk/mission-theology-advisory-group-resources/ and https://www.churchofengland.org/sites/default/files/2017-11/MTAG%2095%20Missional%20Theses_0.pdf

10. By way of contrast, Twitter users who followed us were predominantly clergy and other church leaders.

11. The relative popularity of the theses was determined by reference to the number of retweets or shares in the first 24 hours, and the number of different conversations generated by them. I am indebted to Dr Anne Richards who not only posted the initial statements but has also been responsible for their final editing as well as an extensive analysis of how the theses were received and used.

12. https://schooloftheologynet.files.wordpress.com/2010/07/the-dream-wesley-frensdorff.pdf
The image of Jesus as holy fool has a long history in the Christian tradition: see Elizabeth-Anne Stewart, *Jesus the Holy Fool* (New York: Sheed & Ward 1999). For an account of clowning in ministry, see Roly Bain, *Fools Rush In: a call to Christian clowning* (Grand Rapids: Zondervan 1993); Olive Fleming Drane, *Clowns, Storytellers, Disciples* (Philadelphia: Augsburg 2004).

Is cultural change now so rapid and unpredictable, that our calling is to know how to ask the right questions, to articulate them in simple ways for others, and to walk alongside people as they struggle to make sense of it all?

John Drane

future
present
planet

michael northcott

Introduction

>>I walked here from the centre of
Oxford, because I find walking a
good way to situate oneself in one's
environment and I was curious to
see where the new CMS office was,
having known the old ones in Selly
Oak, Birmingham and in Waterloo,
London. This is in an interesting
place. There's not a lot of nature
between here and the centre of Oxford.
Concreted-over car parks and rather
depressing architecture. As I passed
the Cowley factory of the BMW/Mini
plant, I was really beginning to get
a bit low, actually, and then I found
this lovely shrub overhanging the
Cowley factory, with large amounts of
berries pouring out of it. And then
just past the shrub there was a great
big billboard by the railway bridge
of a lady who was clearly not looking
very happy, and it says something
along the lines maybe you could do
a bit about the environment of the
city to cheer people up! It isn't just
drugs and counselling that's needed in
this part of Oxford, it seems to me.
Maybe also a bit of Christian mission
as well, to some of those rather
tired-looking estates... But who
knows, perhaps it's already going on.

Michael Northcott

Future Present Planet

This is an interesting topic. And that phrase does very much relate in a way to where we currently are, in terms of our relationship with our planet. We are in a new future already, though in the present we are not fully aware of it. This is the hottest year since climate records began that we are living in right now. We have just passed the average of 400 parts per million of CO_2, which is the greenhouse gas in the atmosphere. The earth is warming faster than it has ever warmed in human history. And there is more CO_2 in the atmosphere than there has been – and this is a really hard number to get your head around – for 15 million years, according to the climate record. We can get the record from rocks, essentially – we can tell from the rocks how much CO_2 there was in the atmosphere when the limestone, for example, was deposited in hills.

There were no human beings on earth 15 million years ago. So humanity has never lived on a planet with 400 parts per million CO_2 before. We are rapidly losing the ice as a result. The Northwest Passage is opening up. Ships are regularly going across the Passage now in the summer, increasingly even ones without strengthened hulls.

But there is an enormous time lag. This is why the Future Present metaphor is a helpful one for thinking about climate change. In the present there is enough CO_2 in the atmosphere eventually to melt the ice to get us to there. And then, as you will see, Cambridge will have lost the Boat Race! Because it won't exist any longer; it will be under the sea.

It is possible, I suppose, that we in the UK, and I don't know how long it will take – maybe 200 years – for our descendants to find ways to live. They will rebuild cities. Bristol, Glasgow, most of Edinburgh (where I live), London, will all disappear. Most of the Thames Valley, and the issue of the third runway, will become irrelevant because it will be underwater. People will relocate, but in very large numbers. Hopefully we will still have a functioning economy, having left by that stage the European Union, I suppose. Whether we will still be shipping Minis to Belgium begins to look like a rather irrelevant question, if Belgium doesn't exist anymore.

But if you live in Bangladesh, or in other parts of the developing world, this scenario looks a lot scarier. People are already losing their lands from climate change. On my travels I am reading a book by Amitav Ghosh. He is a wonderful novelist and this book is called *The Great Derangement*. On the cover it has the Brahmaputra Delta, in Bangladesh, from where his parents and grandparents were forced to leave over 100 years ago. Bangladesh will mostly disappear, even with seven metres of sea-level rise, and many millions of people are already homeless because of climate change. But virtually the whole nation of Bangladesh disappears, with the amount of CO_2 we've got in the atmosphere now. It's just a matter of time.

Now, of course, we're all being told that we had this agreement in Paris and how wonderful it was that all the nations of the world agreed. It has been signed into law by many countries in the world in record time, compared to the Kyoto protocol. But unlike the Kyoto protocol there are no legally mandated reductions in CO_2 contained in this treaty. Furthermore, the treaty doesn't contain a reference to what are called fossil fuels. Fossil fuels are plants that synthesise sunlight, turning in the process CO_2 into oxygen, creating conditions for us and our predecessor species to breathe air and live on the earth. And then they were buried in the earth. So it is buried sunlight. We are taking the sunlight out, burning it, and heating up the planet with it. But there is no reference to fossilised plants, to fossil fuels, to coal, oil and gas, in the Paris treaty. Not one single word about coal, oil and gas; or about forests.

So the main causes of climate change on a CO_2 rise are not addressed by the Paris treaty, unfortunately. I wish they were. The Paris treaty only speaks about what are called greenhouse gas emissions, which is what happens when you have taken things out of the ground, when you have turned it into gasolene, when you have put it into an engine or into a furnace in a house, like a gas boiler, and then it goes into the atmosphere. It is a very, very long way along the process. What you have to do, as Bill McKibben a Methodist leader of the 350. org[1] movement has argued for some years, is to stop taking it out of the ground. Unless you do that, it will be burnt. There is no plan in the Paris treaty to stop taking fossil fuels out of the ground.

Climate change, of course, is not the only feature of the environmental crisis that many of us are concerned about. The world is on track, according to a WWF report released just two weeks ago, to lose two thirds of wild animals by 2020 (two thirds of numbers). But growing numbers of species are also threatened with extinction, not just globally, but here in the UK. A friend of mine stayed with me in my garden in Dumfriesshire quite recently – he was quite laid back, and had one of those Harley-Davidson bikes with a great big perspex screen. (Not a Harley, but something like a Harley.) So he sits back in an armchair, and rolls along... he's about 70, though he can still get down a mountain on a pair of skis on a good day... But he said to me, 'You know, the last couple of summers I haven't had to stop and scrape the insects off my perspex screen. They just aren't there anymore.' We've killed them all. We've sprayed the fields so effectively, grown so much wheat etc. in these islands so cheaply, that we are killing all the insects. But what lives off the insects? Birds. What lives off birds - small mammals. What lives off small mammals? Large mammals. We are losing it all. Not just globally, but here in the UK.

In November, many of us wear poppies but I am very concerned about this. Some people, millennials and others, are beginning to say "We need a different kind of Remembrance Day. We need to remember the species that we are losing, and that we have already lost." And 30th November is, for some people, the Remembrance Day for Lost Species.

If you ask what is causing it, then I have talked about the oil and gas industry. Ultimately the oil and gas industry fuels this extraordinary thing called the global economy. This has been an issue in Brexit, it has been an issue in the American election, e.g. should we make everything in China and India and ship it to the UK and sack all the locals or not? Some people would say it is not a terribly good plan. It is certainly not a good plan by Mother Earth. Leaving out nationalistic economics for a moment, it is not a good plan by Mother Earth. The extent now to which the use of our devices depends upon coal wrecking the atmosphere in China or India for example, depends often on slave labour. It is really shocking. But these large global networks – logistic networks, as they are known – hide the impact. If we knew that buying that object was going to wreck the atmosphere in someone's city so their children died young, we wouldn't buy it. But the chains of the global economy are so large that we don't see the way it's enchaining and enslaving our fellow human beings, and enslaving the environment.

But the other thing about this is the sheer power, now, of human beings over the planet. We have become a geological force. A force of nature. We are the first species in the history of the planet to change the climate. All the previous big climate events have occurred through things like large meteorite hits, or volcanic eruptions like Krakatoa. We are the first species to change the conditions of life for everything else on the planet. And we can change the weather.

There are still politicians who say we are not that powerful; we cannot influence the weather. We are changing global systems, like the jet stream, like the Gulf Stream, like the ocean streams which drive the jet streams. And this of course is having terrible human impacts. Every single one of the countries which has had a dramatic decline in rainfall since 1970 has been through a crisis; a political crisis or an economic crisis in the last eight years. Italy, Greece, Spain, Portugal. Then Tunisia, where the so-called Arab Spring turned into an Arab Winter because of the rising fruit prices. Libya. Look at Egypt, Syria, Jordan.

Syria, as we all know, is caught up in a horrendous civil war, where millions have been displaced. I heard from a Christian aid worker at Greenbelt a couple of summers ago that it was sparked by the drought, and Assad gave all the licences to drill for water to the farmers, to his own Alawite people, and denied it to the Sunni majority. And this sparked the civil war, which has had such terrible consequences, and which we're now seeing on the shores of Europe. And to our great shame as a nation, we have turned away thousands of these people, including Syrian, Ethiopian, Afghani children who were waiting to reach relatives here in the UK before the camp was dispersed in Calais.

What we are doing to the Earth is unprecedented. It is certainly unprecedented geologically, but it is even more unprecedented in terms of the history of human civilisation; and in terms of the history of religion, including our Abrahamic religions. These all began in the period of the last 10,000 years, which has been a uniquely stable time in the climate of the Earth. And the climate stability the Earth has enjoyed over the last 10,000 years gave human beings the ability to develop what we call agriculture. Agriculture gave us the division of labour; the ability to store food soon developed.

The story of the storage of food, of course, is famously told towards the end of the book of Genesis. The book of Genesis begins with hunter-gatherers who turn into agrarians, who select plants and get into trouble. The Fall is about plant selection, essentially. And then they are exiled, and they are told they have to plant plants in contest with weeds, and they have to raise their food by the sweat of their brow, and no longer pick it off the trees as they had done before. This is a myth about the transition from hunter-gatherer into agriculture.

What made agriculture possible in the Levant and in China and in the Mayan civilisation, and developed almost simultaneously in central America, the Levant and in China, was climate stability. People could start to grow the grasses they had for many thousands of years previously been plucking wild and milling. I'm sure you've all heard of *The History of the World in 100 Objects*, and the first object in that wonderful series was 60,000-year-old millstones. Yes, but we didn't start selecting the plant until 10,000 years ago. And in a remarkably short time, that ability to select plants gave us priests, temples, monarchs, slaves, civilisation. That's what the first book of the Bible describes.

But by the time that we live in, the extent of influence over the planet that agriculture and then industry have given us, has reached proportions which were completely unimaginable when the Bible was written. The impact of human influence has gone up exponentially in the 20th century, so much so that scientists are now saying that we are living in a new era – a new geological era. The Holocene was the era of the stable climate; the era of agriculture and the development of civilisation. The Anthropocene era is sometimes called the Age of Man, where we are in one way in control of the planet, but in another way we're not in control, because we are not doing these things intentionally – we don't intend to raise the temperature when we turn the gas on at night to warm our homes, or when we build cities on a huge scale.

In the Bible, the first record of human influence on the environment is in Genesis 2 & 3, the second creation story, where it is said that Adam and Eve chose to eat of a tree they were not supposed to eat from, which is why I said it's about plant selection, or inappropriate plant selection. And then they are exiled. And you see in Michelangelo's beautiful depiction of this event (The Exile from Eden), on the Sistine Chapel roof, that on the left Earth looks more verdant and green and luxuriant, and on the right Earth looks less verdant. Exile is going to have an influence, an effect, on nature, and not only on humans.

In my past, I was a missionary in Malaysia. And it was my experiences in Malaysia that turned me into an environmental theologian. And in particular it was a visit I made to this town – the town of Belaga, in Sarawak, Borneo. You can see the river is brown, because the trees are being cut down; the soil which is 10,000 years old is being washed down into the river, and the area floods. People there traditionally lived in longhouses; a number of these longhouses were christianised over the years by Methodists and Anglicans and others, and now the Borneo Inland Mission as it is sometimes called, or the indigenous church in Borneo. And in the longhouses they lived off the jungle without cutting it down. They would cut down small areas to plant fruit trees, but a lot of the food they live off was gathered from the jungle itself.

And these are durians, which are extremely valuable but extremely smelly fruits. I don't know if any of you have ever been in South East Asia, but you're not allowed to take these into hotels because the smell is so strong that if it gets into the air conditioning system you can never get it out again. It smells somewhere like a mix between rotten egg and vanilla ice cream – it's very strange. It's quite addictive and it's also a narcotic, and Malaysians completely love them. So they are very valuable, and you can get US$20 or US$30 for them. So they are very valuable trees.

They also practise a small-scale slash-and-burn type of farming. So they cut an area of forest for six or seven years, plant rice and other staple crops (rice is the staple). I went with my kids on a visit to churches and Christians in that area. I went to a longhouse with my two small children, and I can still remember sitting down and eating wild rice that had been grown. We were not hot; it was cool and the house was traditionally built, traditionally ventilated – it didn't need air conditioning, it didn't need a fan. And they loved it too. I can still remember that visit – it was quite extraordinary.

And yet while we were there, in the town of Belaga, we met a Christian doctor whom we had first met in Sibu, before we came up the great Rajang river. We met her again while we were in Belaga. She had been up in a helicopter visiting far-flung communities of indigenous peoples in this region. She described how they were malnourished, and she was trying to treat the impossible. You can't treat people who are malnourished; they need food; they don't need drugs. I was so shocked by her story, because Borneo is one of the most fertile places on Earth. You don't have to work hard to get your food in Borneo; it's like the Garden of Eden. Food just grows in the trees.

But if you cut the trees down, if you build logging tracks like these, and take the trees away, and sell them corruptly as the Chief Minister did for 25 or more years, you'll not only displace creatures like the orang-utan (which means 'person outside; 'orang' = person; 'utan' = outside/jungle). So in their language they have a real sense that these animals are people like us. And they are like us. They take 5 years to rear their young, and they space their births. They don't have condoms; they just somehow know how to do it. And they only have one, and for those five years the mother and child are very close. It's the longest period of nurture of any other animal than humans. Once the five years are up, and they have been attached virtually the whole time to the mother, you have a strong, stable, psychologically whole adult who can go off and forage and do whatever he or she needs to do to survive for herself. But they are very like us, and the Malay sort of know this.

Michael Northcott

Biblical Vision

But it is not only orang-utans, and other precious creatures, who are being affected by what's going on in Borneo. It's the whole region, and it's the whole planet. I was visiting a former student in the town of Malacca in 2014. I went to sleep one night and woke up the next morning; I was going to preach in the church that day and there was going to be a baptism of my friend Jason's grandson. I had smelt burning in the night, and I'm obviously not very risk-averse, because I woke up briefly and thought, I know Jason likes a glass of whisky but I didn't think he smokes. I went back to sleep.

In the morning, I opened the curtains and I couldn't see down the street. There was haze and smoke, and it smelt like a bonfire. Now Malacca is only 20 miles from Sumatra, and Sumatra was on fire that day. Once they have burned the region they turn it into an oil palm; often it is oil palm plantations who sub-contract the burning. But the burning is estimated to kill thousands of people a year in south-east Asian cities. And in one particularly bad year they reckoned that 30,000 people died from the smoke.

It's truly appalling; it is a human tragedy, the environmental crisis. It is not only about trees and orang-utans and forests; it is about human beings. It is about people who have formed barricades on the logging route, and who have tried to stop it, and then get arrested by police for disturbing the peace. It is very troubling, and it was very troubling for me to experience this. But as a result of the experience of visiting these people, I thought that as an academic I would devote my career to teaching my students about the connection between Christian faith and what we sometimes call care for creation. And for me perhaps the crucial text which in the Old Testament sums up the connection between Christian mission and salvation and care for the Earth is the last part of Isaiah 65:

For I am about to create a new heavens and a new earth; the former things shall not be remembered or come to mind, but be glad and rejoice for ever in what I am creating.

I am about to create Jerusalem as a joy and its people a delight. And I will rejoice in Jerusalem and delight in my people who shall no more hear the sound of weeping in it or the cry of distress; no more shall there be an infant who lives but a few days or an old person who does not live out a lifetime. For one who dies at a hundred years will be considered a youth; the one who falls short of a hundred will be considered accursed. (Isa 65:17-20)

To me, this is the first statement in human history of what we now call development. It's about infant mortality rates; it's about mortality rates; it's about longevity. People in the UK are now living to 100. Not all of them, but some of them. Many people are living to 90 – I have two relatives who are over 90. I have had five relatives who were over 90 when they died, and two are still alive.

But it is also about a sustainable economy, a local economy, an economy where people have a stake – not like the one where the Germans own the trains and the French own the hotel I stayed in last night, and all the rest of it.

They shall build houses and inhabit them; they shall plant vineyards and eat their fruit. They shall not build, and another inhabit; they shall not plant, and another eat. For like the days of a tree shall the days of my people be, and my chosen shall long enjoy the work of their hands. They shall not labour in vain, or bear children for calamity, for they shall be offspring blessed by the Lord, and their descendants as well. Before they call, I will answer; while they are yet speaking, I will hear.' (Isa 65:21-24)

This vision of peace, this vision of human development, the first I would say in human history, is absolutely essential to the biblical conception which occurs at the end of the prophet Isaiah, of when the salvation which was first promised to the Jews overspills to all people on the planet, which of course we believe it did in the coming of Christ. For Isaiah it doesn't only overspill to all people. Famously, he concludes, it overspills to all creatures.

And, yes, in some ways it's an impossible dream by this point. 'The wolf and the lamb shall feed together' – well, not unless the wolf has some serious psychological re-training. 'The lion shall eat straw like the ox' – well, could a lion live off grass? Could a lion become a vegetarian? Again, probably, but not without a lot of training. 'But the serpent's food shall be dust' – ah, so the serpent is still connected to the Fall. 'But, they shall not hurt or destroy in all my holy mountain, says the Lord.' (Isa 65:24-25)

And this of course is Edward Hicks' famous painting of Isaiah's vision, called *The Peaceable Kingdom*. In the background of the painting you have a treaty being made by the people of the city of Philadelphia and the native American tribes in that part of the United States: a treaty that is said to have been kept, unlike all of

Edward Hicks, Peaceable Kingdom, c. 1834
Courtesy National Gallery of Art, Washington

the others. And in the foreground the lion is eyeing supper, but deciding to forgo the privilege.

People say but this is all very Old Testament; Jesus wasn't an environmentalist; where is this in the New Testament? Where is this in our part of the Bible? (Yes, there are a few Marcionites, I find sometimes, in evangelical and Catholic circles...!) Well, look at the New Testament. There is the famous story of the stilling of the storm on the sea of Galilee, beautifully depicted in the wonderful narrative painting by Rembrandt (which is actually in a private museum in Boston). Jesus was asleep in the stern, as is famously told, on a pillow; the disciples are afraid of losing their lives. They wake him up; he gets up and says "What's all the fuss about?" And then he rebuked the wind and said to the waves, "Quiet! Be still." And the wind died down and it was completely calm. And he said to his disciples, "Why are you so afraid? Do you not have faith?" They were terrified, and asked each other, "Who is this? Even the wind and the waves obey him.'"

The Lord of the universe was born in flesh and blood. The new relationship with the creation began in Jesus Christ. The reconciliation that was long overdue and long promised between human beings and the earth, that began in the exile from Eden, begun again in Jesus Christ.

And that's why, in the story of the Passion, in the course of the crucifixion, very close to his death, we read that there was an eclipse. Even the earth responded to the death of Christ. 'It was now about noon, and darkness came over the whole land until three in the afternoon. And while the sun's light failed, the curtain of the temple was torn in two.' (Luke 23:44-45) The old religion that had divided the world between Jew and Gentile was over. The old covenant was over. Reconciliation between human beings and the earth was just beginning. The earth knew it before the human beings. 'And Jesus, crying with a loud voice, said, "Father, into thy hands I commend my spirit."' (Luke 23:46)

The early Christians, I think, got this. They knew that the new creation was a cosmic, and not only a human event. St Paul uses the phrase quite early on in his letter to the Corinthians: 'If anyone is in Christ, there is a new creation; everything old has passed away...' He speaks about how we are ambassadors for Christ, and our work is a work of reconciliation. But it's very clear in the epistles of St Paul that it's a cosmic reconciliation he has in mind, not only human but one that embraces the whole history of the planet of peoples and species.

And yet so often in our Christian culture we don't get this cosmic dimension of salvation. I wrote a paper a few years ago on the *Left Behind*[2] series (you might wonder what a scholar was doing reading those novels!). But we were driving home from Suffolk one time and I was dropped off at my wife's cousin's house, and she was chucking out the whole lot. She had them all – she was quite evangelical, she had read 20 novels, and they were all hardbacks. I don't know – on a whim I said I'll take them – it might be an interesting project!

And I did – I read through them, fairly quickly (there was some pretty weird stuff!), just seeing what is nature in these books. And nature was just the background for machines, the machines that enable those who were left behind but became saints after the Rapture to fight the good fight. It's an extraordinary vision; a very strange set of books; but it's been incredibly influential in the evangelical world in USA, and I think quite a lot of people have read them here, too. Mother Earth is just not in the picture except as a sort of backdrop to be fought. Earth simply punishes the saints, and the saints only survive because of their technology and ingenuity.

I lived for a short time in the community L'Abri founded by Francis Schaeffer in the 1950s in Switzerland, and another one here in England. He famously wrote a book called *Pollution and the Death of Man: the Christian view of ecology* in 1968. And he argued in that book that Christians ought to 'get' the ecological crisis; it wasn't just hippies, it wasn't just people going to Woodstock; people like Joni Mitchell and Neil Young, who ought to get it. He was saying, No, we all ought to get this, and we evangelical Christians ought to get it most of all. Because the earth is God's creation; it is destined to be redeemed, and its redemptive form bears a resemblance to its current physical characteristics. And so we ought to defend these from abuse and excessive manipulation.

We find something very similar in Pope Francis' encyclical on the environment *Laudato Si*. The New Testament doesn't only tell us of Jesus and his loving relationship with the world; it shows him risen and glorious – present, throughout creation. 'For in him all the fullness of the godhead was pleased to dwell, to reconcile to himself all things in heaven and earth, making peace by the blood of his cross.' (Col 1:19-20) And so the Pope concludes: 'The creatures of this world no longer appear to us under merely a natural guise, because the Risen One is mysteriously holding them to himself, and directing them towards fullness as their end.'[3]

Missional Perspective

How to bring this, though, into mission? One way is through Christian architecture, through art, through prayer, through preaching, through theology, and worship. We can depict a new relation to creation. Take the church of St Gregory of Nazianzus in San Francisco that I visited last summer. They have 150 dancing saints around the beautiful lantern-style roof of their church. And the church is like a cosmological building which represents the new creation in its built form. But look what it says in the top of the lantern: 'The one thing truly worthwhile is becoming God's friend.'

This is not some kind of weird, orthodox, unapproachable message that is being put out. I was very moved by the worship in this church, as well as by its art. There was a lot of movement around; they didn't all sit in one place in pews; different parts of the service occurred in different places; there was dancing, there was music, there was liturgy, there was preaching, and the Word had its proper place. And there were also images of other creatures, including this rather wonderful dancing bear. And the people were also imaged, too, in these very lovely rainbow-coloured badges that they all wear on Sunday. (Even as a visitor you get to put one on.)

Now let us visit a place called Possilpark in Glasgow. It is one of the poorest places in Europe, a place of utter ugliness and desolation. It makes Blackbird Leys look beautiful by comparison. I've never seen so much rubbish lying on streets and fields. When I was shown around by the pastor of Clay Community Church that I was visiting, he took me to some of the wild places (you can see some of the flats in the distance), and running through this area there is a 70-acre wild area that was rather messed up and forgotten. Some of the working men keep pigeons in pigeon lofts there – it's their kind of hobby. But Paul Ede and others have got together and formed a group called Friends of Possilpark Greenspace, and tried to turn this space back into a community resource so everyone can share in it. And the Church of St Matthew's, an Episcopal church in Possilpark, has been turned into a community centre.

There are lots of different organisations there: arts, and counselling, and Possilpark Greenspace – all have their little offices and desks, and in the grounds of St Matthew's and they have got community gardens growing there. My friend Paul Ede has established a church there. At the heart of the church, in this very poor community, and this is a classic street-front church which through the week is a counselling centre and all kinds of other things, but on a Sunday the worship is very creation-centred, but also centred on the people, because Paul knows that if you get people back in touch with creation, with the environment, with nature, it's a source of wonder, and of life, and of wholeness that will help them to escape the dreadful depression, the drug addiction that I saw among so many people in that community. It will help them to recover. It's not an escape, of course, because the creation is the theatre of God's glory. It was John Calvin who said in the first volume of the *Institutes*, Book 5: 'If you go to the city, you see human corruption. If you go to Nature, you still see the work of God.' And Paul gets that. That's why the Clay Community Church is basically a green church.[4]

If you want to do this in the churches, the pioneering missions that you are involved with, you might find some help by going to A Rocha UK, a charity of which I am a patron. It has recently set up Eco Church to replace something called Eco Congregations. They are trying to resource a very profound reconnection between Christian mission and worship and care for creation as a way of demonstrating that the gospel of good news for God's people is also good news for God's earth.

Bio:

Michael Northcott is Emeritus Professor of Ethics in the School of Divinity at Edinburgh University and currently Guest Professor at the Faculty of Theology of the University of Heidelberg.

Endnotes:

1. https://350.org/

2. http://leftbehind.com/

3. http://w2.vatican.va/content/francesco/en/encyclicals/documents/papa-francesco_20150524_enciclica-laudato-si.html; 100.

4. http://www.claychurch.org.uk/author/paul-ede/

The earth is God's creation; it is destined to be redeemed, and its redemptive form bears a resemblance

to its current physical characteristics. And so we ought to defend these from abuse and excessive manipulation.

Michael Northcott

afterword:
there
are new
mountains

cathy ross

>>I hope you have enjoyed the journey
- whether you have read all there
is here or just dipped in and out.
Perhaps the FuturePresent metaphor
has captured your imagination and
enabled you to dream of making a
better world now, of being part
of God's Kingdom, of spotting its
presence - perhaps in surprising
places. Perhaps you resonated with how
to innovate, or how to reimagine and
reconfigure our prisons (as well as
our imaginations!), or what church's
physical space could look like, or the
riddles of mission, or experimenting
with imagining Christ as a girl,
or relishing a new relationship to
creation; whatever it was we hope
that these ideas and practices can
encourage you to think, act, speak
boldly, creatively, imaginatively
exercising the gift of sight to see
and envision what a new world could
look like.

Perhaps it just begins with the courage to speak up and speak out; to share
our personal stories, to verbalise our dreams – maybe that is the beginning of
making new worlds.

A powerful example of this for me recently was Oprah Winfrey's acceptance
speech at the Golden Globes. The first black woman to receive an award at the
Golden Globes – in 2018! Are we shocked by that? Her speech gave me hope
that patriarchy, racism, sexism and silencing of women are being exposed and
will be forced to change. Oprah thanked all those women who felt strong enough
and empowered to share their stories and she declared "this year we became
the story." Movingly, she thanked the women who had endured years of abuse

and assault. Now women are speaking out about sexual abuse and harassment in many public institutions – the entertainment industry and media, government, education and social services, the church. It is endemic and embedded. Dare we hope that the silencing of women, the patronising of women is being exposed, named, shamed and addressed. Might this lead us into a FuturePresent world?

"That's an excellent suggestion, Miss Triggs. Perhaps one of the men here would like to make it."

Well, yes and no.

Women are speaking out but it is complicated. Nearly thirty years ago, cartoonist Riana Duncan superbly portrayed the sexist attitude that exists in meetings. I have not spoken to a single woman who does not resonate with this cartoon. Not only does she resonate, she then goes on to tell me of instances (sometimes many) when exactly this has happened to her - in 2018! Moreover, when women do speak out, there can be a violent and nasty backlash of abuse or more subtle ways of rendering women incompetent or looking foolish. Let me remind you of two recent examples.

In 2013 the Bank of England announced that Winston Churchill would replace social reformer, Elizabeth Fry on the £5 note. This meant that every bank note issued would have a man on the reverse side – all male luminaries. Caroline Criado-Perez decided to challenge this and naively assumed that the Bank would cave in immediately as it was so clearly an unnecessary and unhelpful decision.This campaign ran for three months with petitions, legal challenges, meetings until finally the Bank gave in and announced that they were issuing a new £10 note with Jane Austen on it. The campaigners had won. However, the day after the Bank's announcement, Caroline received her first rape threat by Twitter. And then another. And another. By the end of the first weekend the police had 300 A4 pages of vitriolic and vicious threats against her. Her (incorrect) address and phone number were posted on the internet. She had a panic button installed in her flat. After two months of constant abuse, she closed down her Twitter account.

Or think of the two ridiculous interviews given by Labour MP Diane Abbott and Tory MP Boris Johnson during the 2017 election campaign. Both of the interviews were embarrassing and displayed ignorance of party policies. The response to the two interviews was revealing. Abbott was mocked and ridiculed for her interview with insults such as "numpty" and "fat idiot". Johnson too was criticised but in a far more friendly way with comments on his laddish behaviour, or that this is just Boris and to get a grip.

Criado-Perez did some research on this phenomenon of silencing and insulting women. In her book she quotes a study from the University of Maryland where fake accounts were set up and sent into chatrooms. "Those with female names received an average of 100 messages every day that included sexually explicit or threatening language."[1] Criado-Perez concludes that women are being told to shut up and be silent. She theorises that many of the threats that she received and much of the violence perpetrated against women focuses around the speech area. Research conducted by Professor Lorna Martin of the University of Cape Town into the injuries suffered by femicide victims found that a large proportion of the injuries were in the face and neck area. Criado-Perez sees this as a clear message – that women are to be shut up by any means necessary. She claims that this silencing starts early – boys interrupt at almost three times the rate of girls according to some research.

Mary Beard uncovers the double standard that women suffer from in her excellent book, *Women and Power*. She writes, "It is not just that it is more difficult for women to succeed; they get treated much more harshly if they ever mess up. Think Hillary Clinton and those emails."[2] In her carefully argued book she considers the public voice of women and how difficult it is for women to be heard in the public sphere. She argues that culturally, we are hard-wired not to hear women.

Beard also asserts that when a woman offers views that are different or controversial, she is considered stupid. She writes that she has "lost count of the number of times I've been called an 'ignorant moron.'"[3] Another example of this is in Michael Kimmel's great TED talk on gender equality where he tells the story of presenting a guest lecture on a female colleague's course. As he walks in, one of the students looks up and says "Oh finally, an objective opinion"![4] By contrast, I recently remarked to a (male) colleague that I could not understand how a particular man had remained head of a large organisation for so long when he seemed to me so blusteringly incompetent. My colleague replied, "I can tell you in three words. White. Male. Middle-class." Is he right? Is this a generally accurate diagnosis I wondered? Well, is he? Is it? You can decide.

Beard challenges us to think about what we mean by the "voice of authority" and how we construct it. She also challenges us to reconsider what we mean by power. She claims that power, as it is currently constructed and experienced is "coded as male"[5] so that we need to change the structure and to think about power differently. How often have you had that conversation with other women? She is, and this is where we get onto our FuturePresent theme, "a little" optimistic about change although she remains "gloomy" overall. Personally, I think patriarchy is so embedded that I wonder if it will ever disappear before the new creation, but I do see signs of hope. Women finding their voices and speaking out is one sign of that change.

I read a marvellous expression of this by Ursula Le Guin in Rebecca Solnit's (currently one of my favourite essayists) latest book, *The Mother of All Questions, Further Feminisms*: "We are volcanoes. When we women offer our experience as truth, as human truth, all the maps change. There are new mountains."[6] I see this happening. Sexual gratification and abuse has been outed in the entertainment industry. Unequal pay has long been on the agenda but the ongoing iniquity of the gender pay gap has been clearly highlighted by the recent resignation of Carrie Gracie, China Editor at the BBC. The Equality Act 2010 (note it has taken until the 21st century!) states that men and women doing equal work must receive equal pay. Last July Gracie learned that her two male counterparts earned at least 50% more than she and her female counterpart. In her open letter to the BBC audience, she wrote:

*Despite the BBC's public insistence that my appointment demonstrated its
commitment to gender equality, and despite my own insistence that equality
was a condition of taking up the post, my managers had yet again judged that
women's work was worth much less than men's. My bewilderment turned
to dismay when I heard the BBC complain of being forced to make these pay
disclosures. Without them, I and many other BBC women would never have
learned the truth.*[7]

This is discrimination and it is illegal. It beggars belief that anyone in the BBC
management could find this acceptable. Hard-wired indeed. But Gracie spoke
out and took a symbolic action so this gives us hope.

Oprah said that for too long women had not been believed when they spoke
truth to the power of men but "their time is up. Their time is up!" She believes a
new day is on the horizon where women will not need to say #metoo and where
men will choose to listen. This is the world we were dreaming about at our
FuturePresent Day. Let us leave behind the old world, which is in bondage to sin
and brokenness that keeps us apart, diminished and less than human. Let us
dream dreams, be bold and become the new creation that we can be in Christ.

Women are speaking up and speaking out. There are seeds of hope. I believe,
that as the angel said to Mary, "with God, all things are possible." And in line with
Mary's story, we are required to be courageous, to take those first steps into a
sometimes unknown and uncomfortable landscape, and to imagine a completely
new world where power is reconstructed, where all voices are heard and valued
and where there are new mountains and maps can be changed.

Bio:

Dr Cathy Ross is MA Coordinator for Pioneer Leadership Training at CMS
(Church Mission Society) and Tutor in Contextual Theology at Ripon College
Cuddesdon. She has edited several books on mission and her research interests
are in the areas of contextual theologies, World Christianity, feminist theologies
and hospitality. She is married to Steve, a GP in Oxford and they have three
children and two grandchildren. She enjoys tennis, swimming, coffee, travel and
watching the All Blacks.

Endnotes:

1. Caroline Criado-Perez, *Do it Like a Woman... and change the world*, (London:Portobello, 2015), 124.

2. Mary Beard, *Women and Power, A Manifesto*, (London:Profile Books, 2017), 96.

3. Ibid, 33.

4. https://www.youtube.com/watch?v=7n9IOH0NvyY, accessed 12.01.2018.

5. Beard, *Women*, 87.

6. Quoted in Rebecca Solnit, *The Mother of All Questions, Further Feminisms*, (London:Granta,2017), 18.

7. https://www.theguardian.com/media/2018/jan/08/carrie-gracie-letter-in-full, accessed 12.01.2018

We hope that these ideas and practices can encourage you to think, act, speak boldly, creatively, imaginatively exercising the gift of sight to see and envision what a new world could look like.

Cathy Ross

ULTIMATELY

IN ABS

STICK

IT SO

THE

WITH

ONLY

CIRCLE

YOU,

EVERYWHERE

LOVE

TODAY.

ANSWER

I

MANKIN

PROBLEMS.

STRO

ABOUT

A DEMAN

GO.

LOVE

Magenta

I hold the large key, ancient, iron, trefoil,
Cold to touch.
It slides easily into the lock
Turns smoothly.
No creaks for this door. Well oiled.

A tiny chapel
Hidden on a rocky outcrop in north Wales.
Sunlight rainbows in reflected by the stained glass windows.
Seven of them.
Purple, yellow, blue, orange,
Green, red, turquoise, magenta.

Eight colours.
Seven stained glass windows.
Magenta is missing.
Where is magenta? worries my tidy mind.

Slowly I absorb the sound of the refracted colours.
Red for strength; green for healing,
Purple for longing, yellow for curiosity,
Orange for vitality, blue for tranquillity,
Turquoise for sheer beauty.

Magenta for completion.

Eight colours on the wheel,
Seven windows in this chapel.

Magenta for completion,
Wholeness.

Magenta is missing.

Magenta calls me on,
Out of the chapel,
Into the world.

St Beuno's, 12 Aug, 2017.

A Proost publication
www.proost.co.uk
Printed by Park Communications

ISBN 978-1-5272-2321-9

Editors: Cathy Ross, Jonny Baker, Steve Collins
Design: Steve Collins

Photo credits:

Ian Adams: pages 25-33
Jonny Baker: pages 5, 76, 130, 142
Steve Collins: cover, pages 10-11, 22, 48-49, 68-69, 90, 106, 160-161, 170-171
Colin Heber-Percy: page 88
Virginia Vlamink: pages 114-117

Image pages 154-155 courtesy National Gallery of Art, Washington
Cartoon page 164 ©2018, Punch Ltd. All Rights Reserved

Additional information:

This book derives from 'FuturePresent', a Pioneer Conversations Day held on 8th November 2016 at Church Mission Society in Oxford.

For more about Pioneer Mission and the CMS Pioneer Mission Leadership Training Course see: https://pioneer.churchmissionsociety.org/

For more about Church Mission Society see: https://churchmissionsociety.org

FITTING IN IS

Put your *pioneer call* into action

OVER-RATED

THESE UNIQUE COURSES **PROVIDE A DYNAMIC COMMUNITY OF PIONEERS DREAMING OF HOW TO MAKE THE FUTURE PRESENT, HOW TO MAKE ANOTHER WORLD POSSIBLE.**

The focus is on **equipping pioneers for innovative mission**

CHURCH MISSION SOCIETY

pioneer.churchmissionsociety.org